God's Inspirations Publishing By: Dishman & Dobbs

125 Bean Street, Monticello, Ky 42633

Copyright© 2015, God's Inspirations Publishing Co.

Written By: Angela Dobbs

Trade Paperback Release: October, 2015

Electric Release: October, 2015 Warning All Rights Reserved The

www.Godsinspirationspublishing.weebly.com.

Angeladobbs5@gmail.com

preacherwoman@windstream.net

This is a work of fiction. Any resemblances to any names, places, or

Incidents are purely coincidental " ANIMALS OF THE WILD COLORING AND ACTIVITY BOOK"

ISBN-13: 978- 1518620959

ISBN-10: 1518620957

Dedication

To my husband, all my family, friends and all the little animal lovers out there!

Acknowledgement

Images provided by: Google.com and Bing.com

ANIMALS OF THE WILD COLORING AND ACTIVITY BOOK

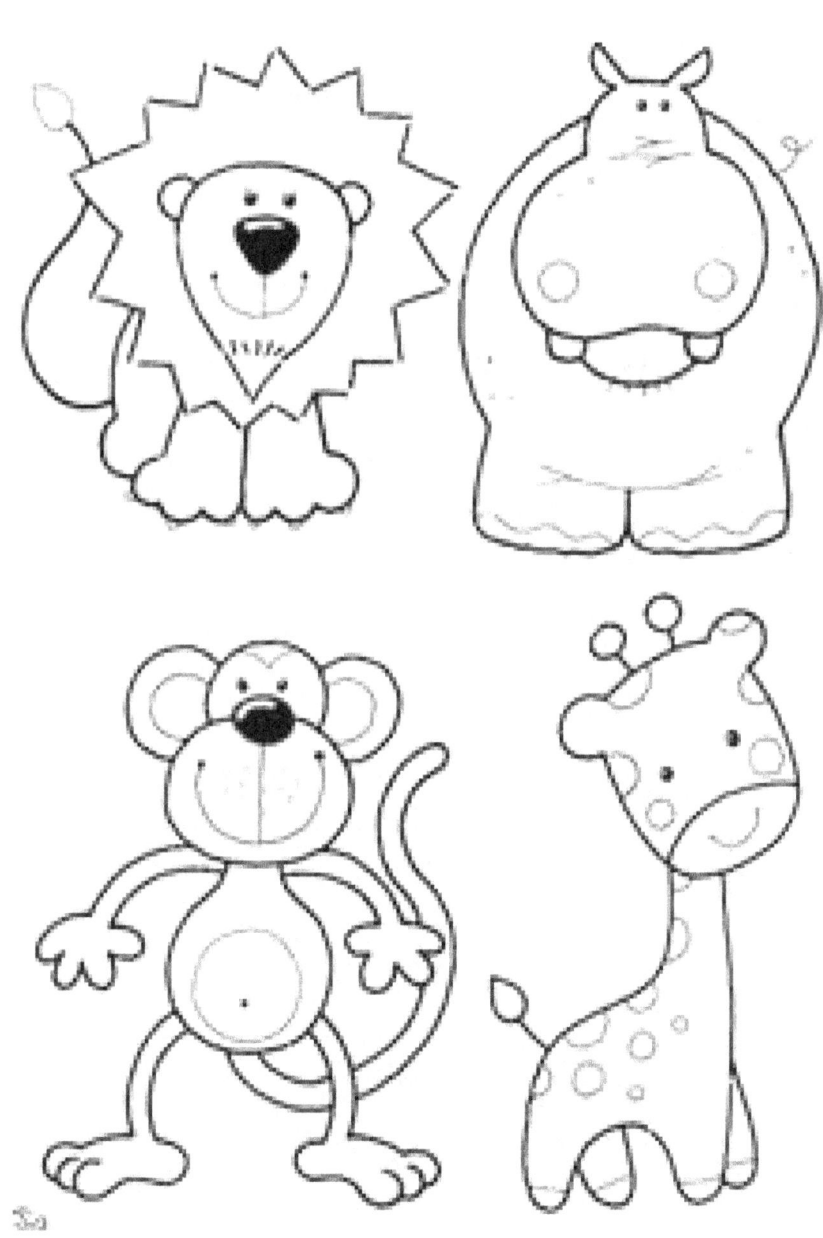

ANIMAL WORD SEARCH

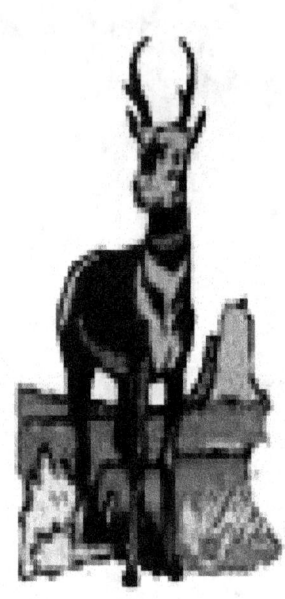

D	A	J	S	R	E	P	T	I	L	E	S	S	E	T
M	G	N	U	C	M	A	T	E	I	C	D	G	A	M
H	A	R	T	N	E	E	H	O	G	R	A	T	H	N
I	W	M	A	L	G	N	N	E	I	R	I	F	S	O
B	H	P	M	S	E	L	T	B	O	B	S	L	F	C
E	I	R	W	A	S	R	E	F	A	E	I	L	U	T
R	S	E	I	O	L	L	S	H	R	A	M	V	R	U
N	K	Y	S	F	L	S	A	O	T	T	L	X	S	R
A	E	Z	Z	W	S	E	V	N	B	C	E	D	E	N
T	R	U	D	E	T	I	T	F	D	A	L	E	Z	A
L	S	R	V	A	N	N	U	B	O	S	B	A	T	L
A	P	O	R	R	U	V	A	L	S	R	R	I	W	H
J	O	G	A	H	P	A	W	S	I	M	E	X	E	S
H	I	C	Z	I	N	S	T	I	N	C	T	S	X	S
M	J	Z	H	E	R	B	I	V	O	R	E	S	T	W

ANTLERS	HERBIVORES	NOCTURNAL
BABIES	HIBERNATE	PAWS
BIRDS	HOOVES	PREY
CARNIVORES	HUNT	PROWL
CLAWS	INSTINCT	REPTILES
FORAGE	JUNGLE	SCENT
FOREST	MAMMALS	TAILS
FUR	MATE	TEETH
GRASSLANDS	MIGRATE	WHISKERS
HABITAT		

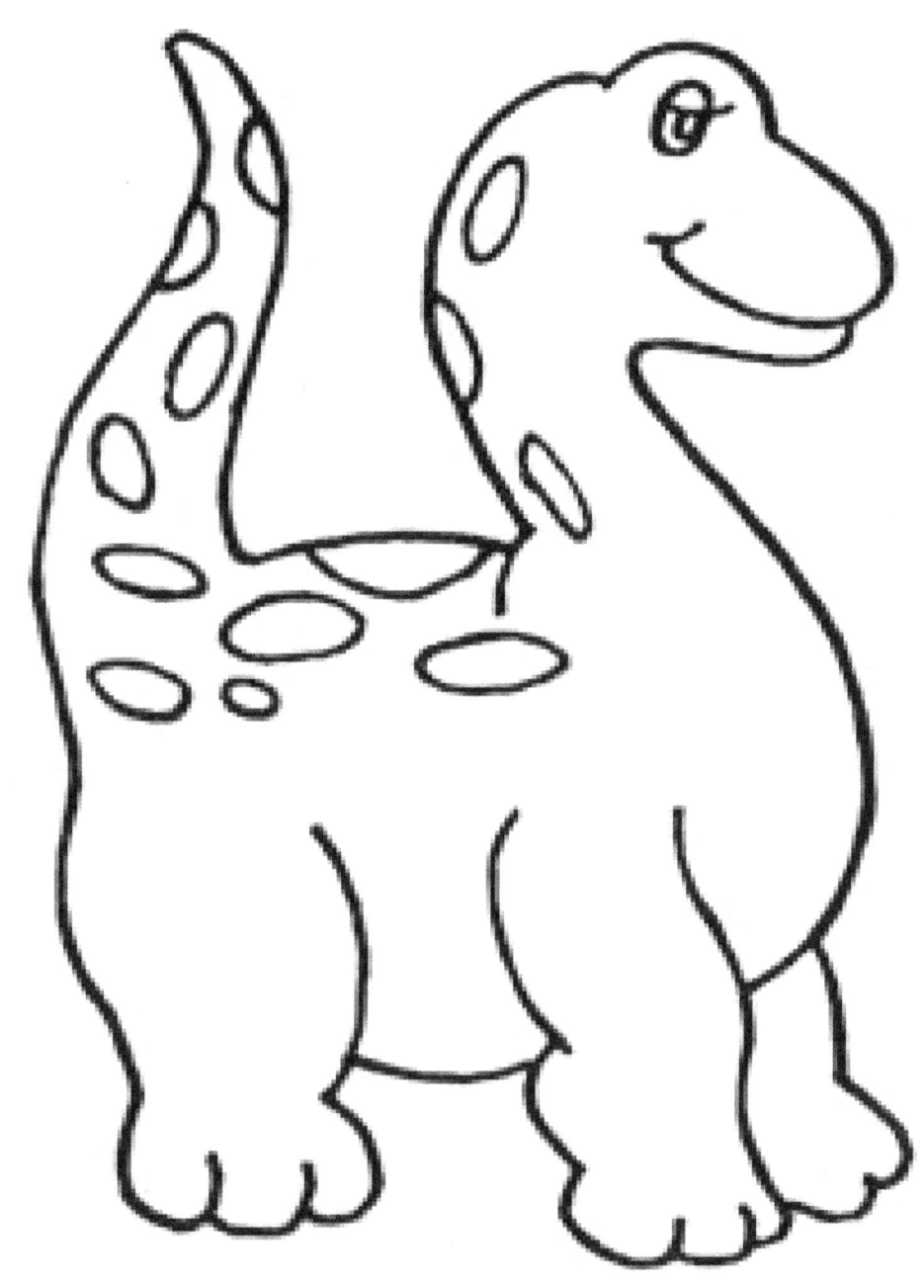

RUSTY THE DINO!!!
WHAT SOUND DOES HE MAKE?

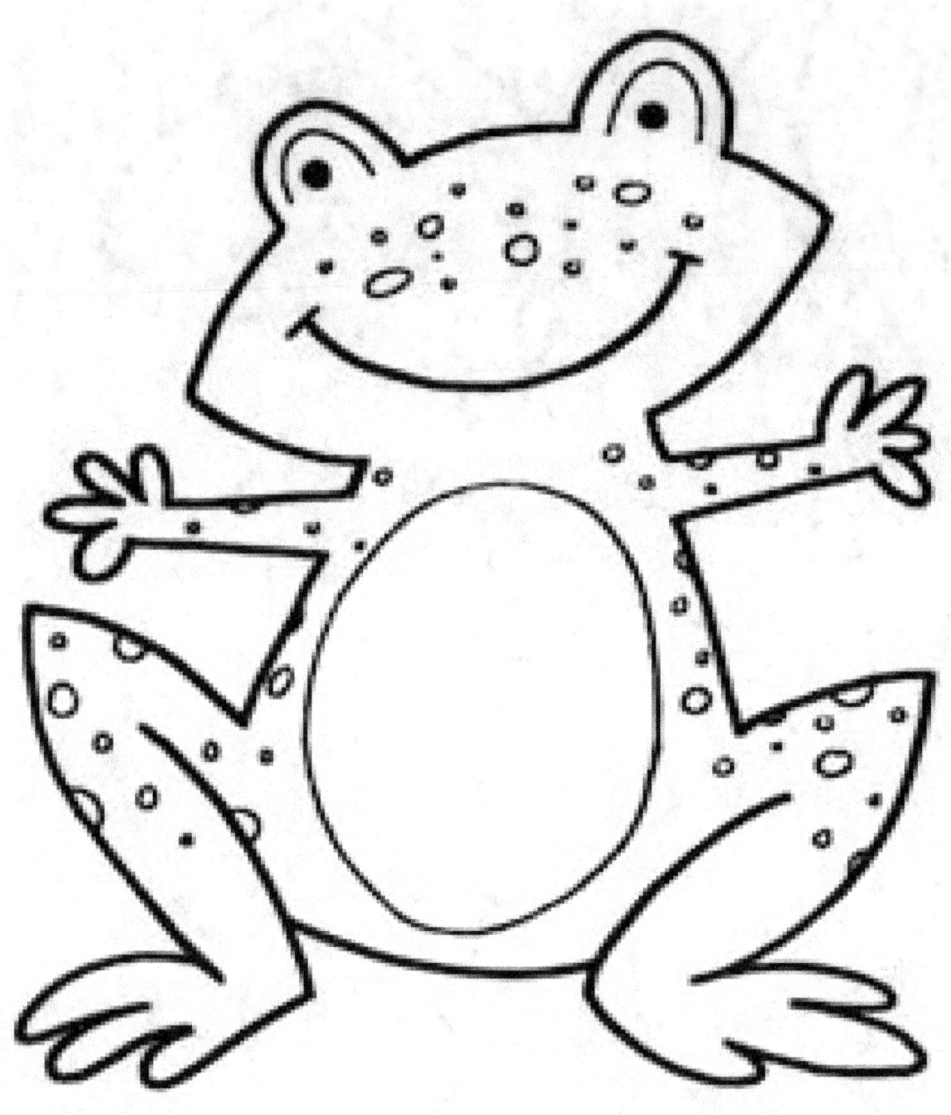

Hello My Name is Frisky the frog!

My sound Is Rib-it Rib-it!

What is you name?

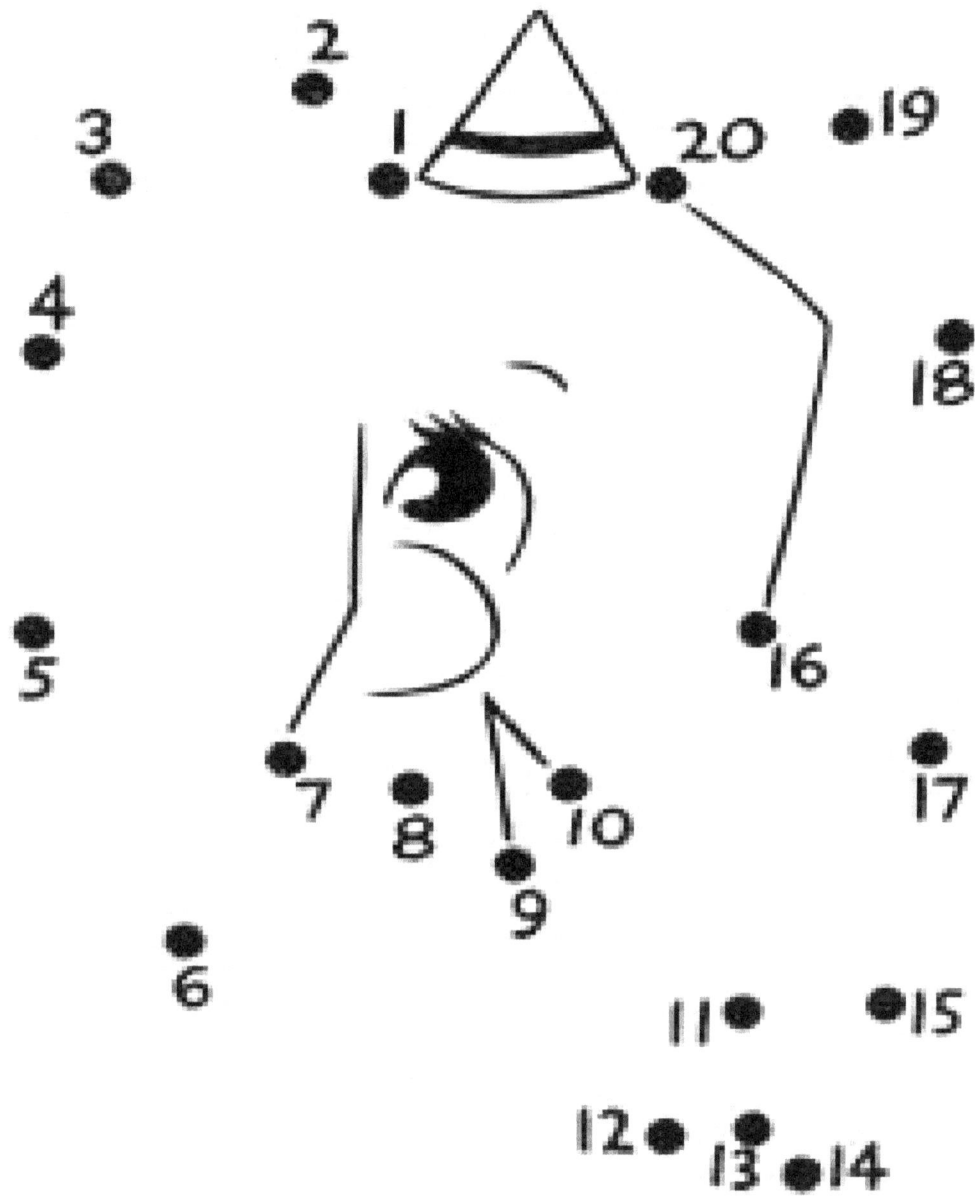

Connect my dots to see who I am!

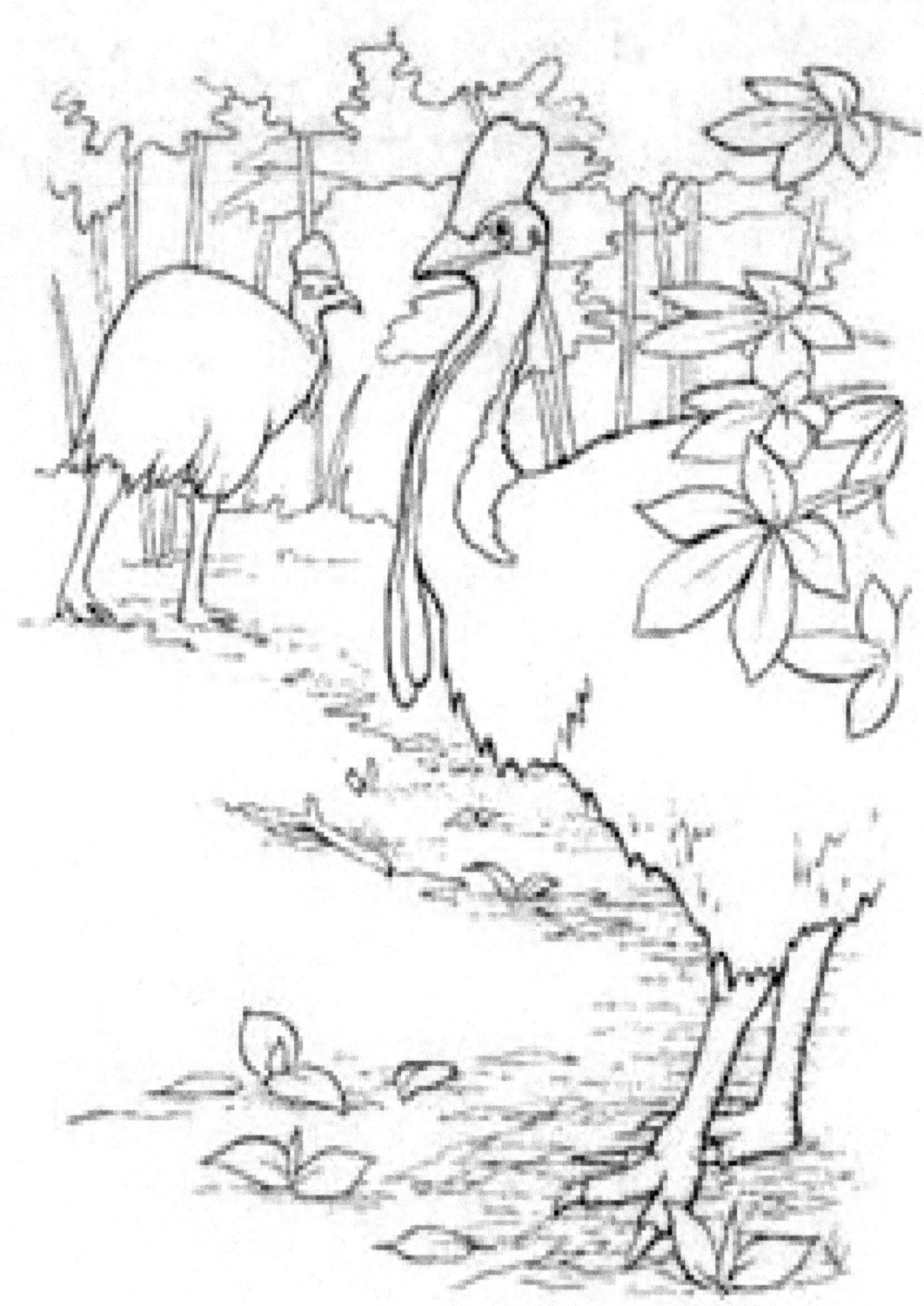

How to draw wild animals

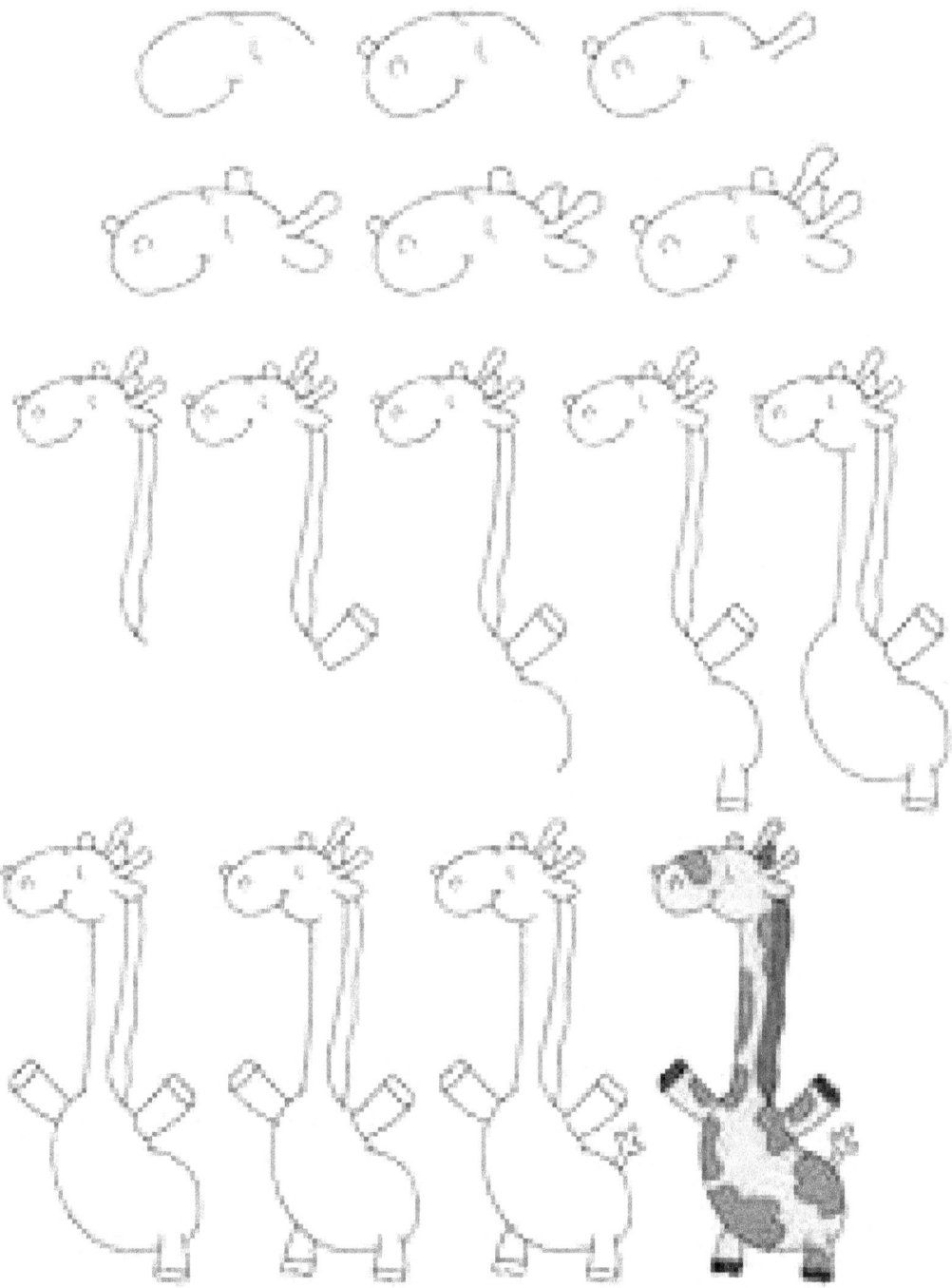

On the next page see if you can draw!

DRAW ANY THING YOU WANT!

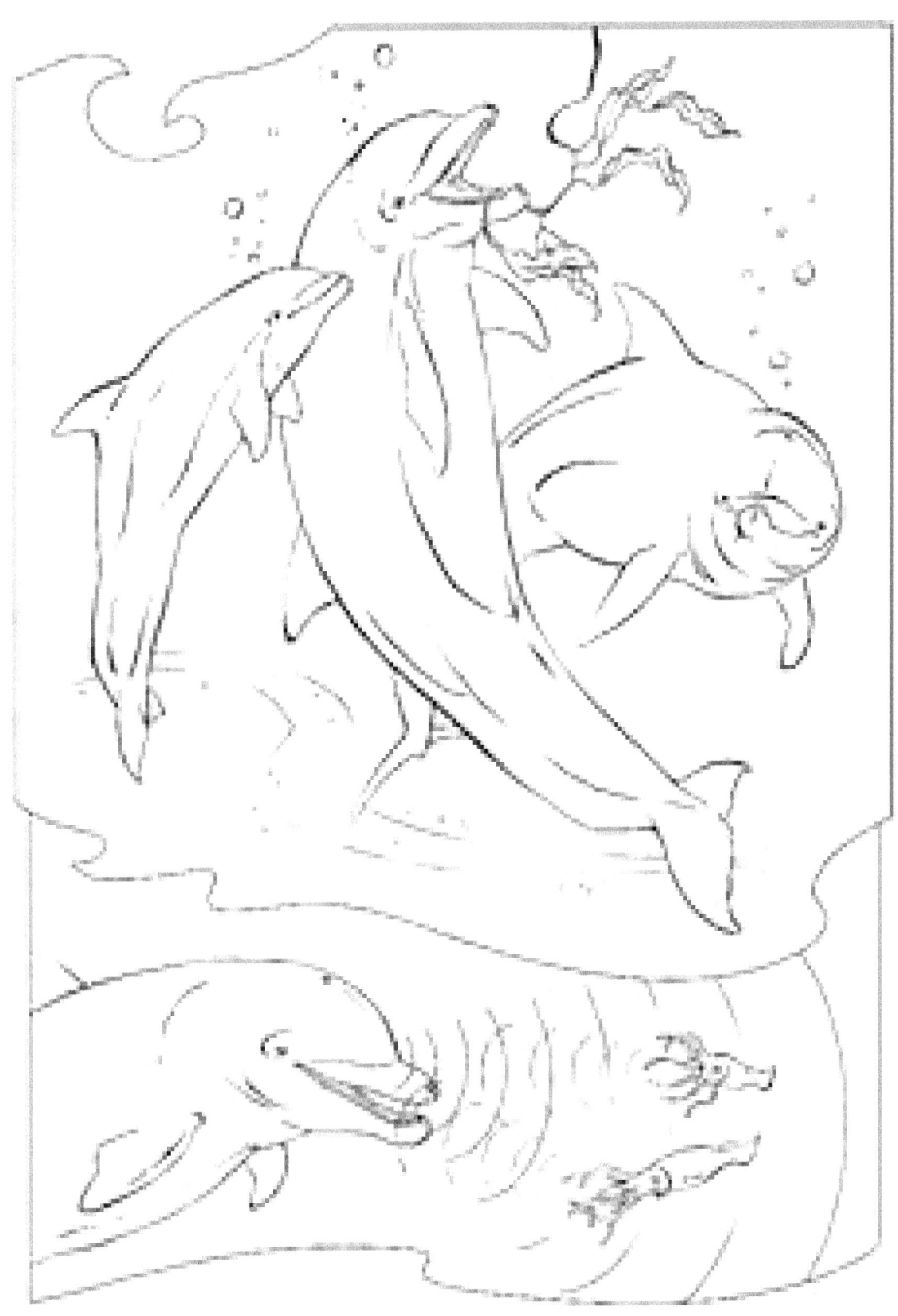

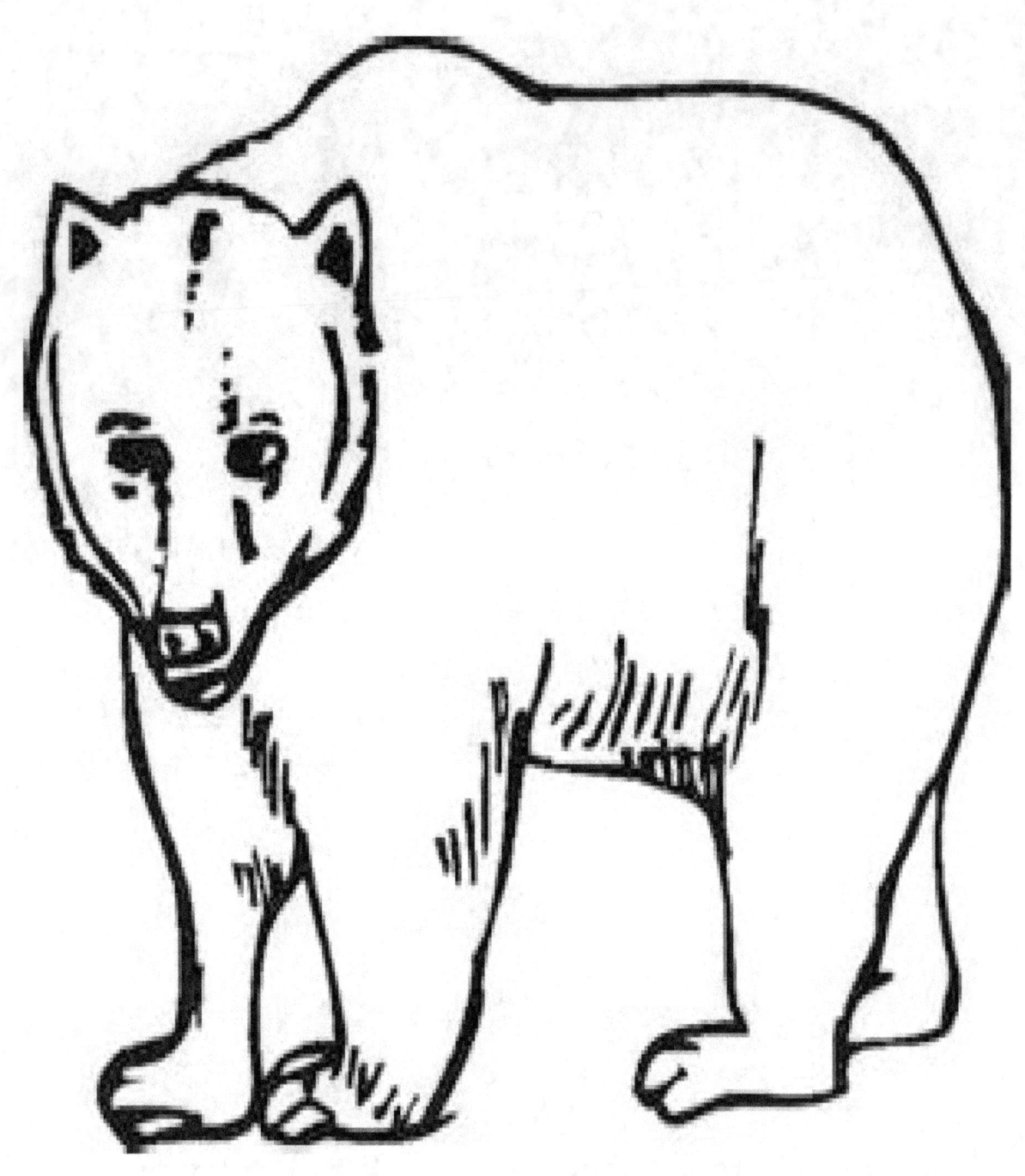

This is Lola Color her Black !

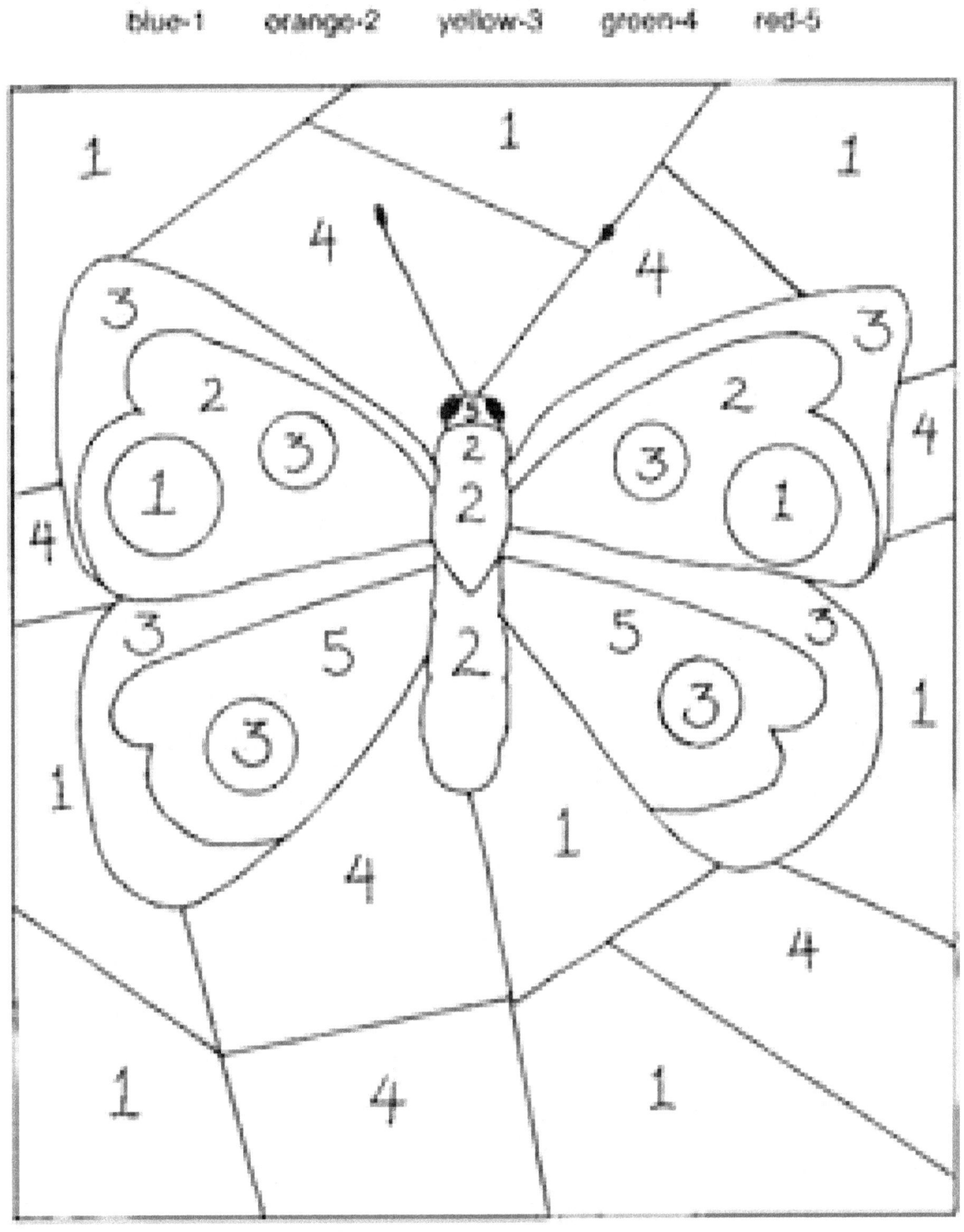

Color by number see the surprise!

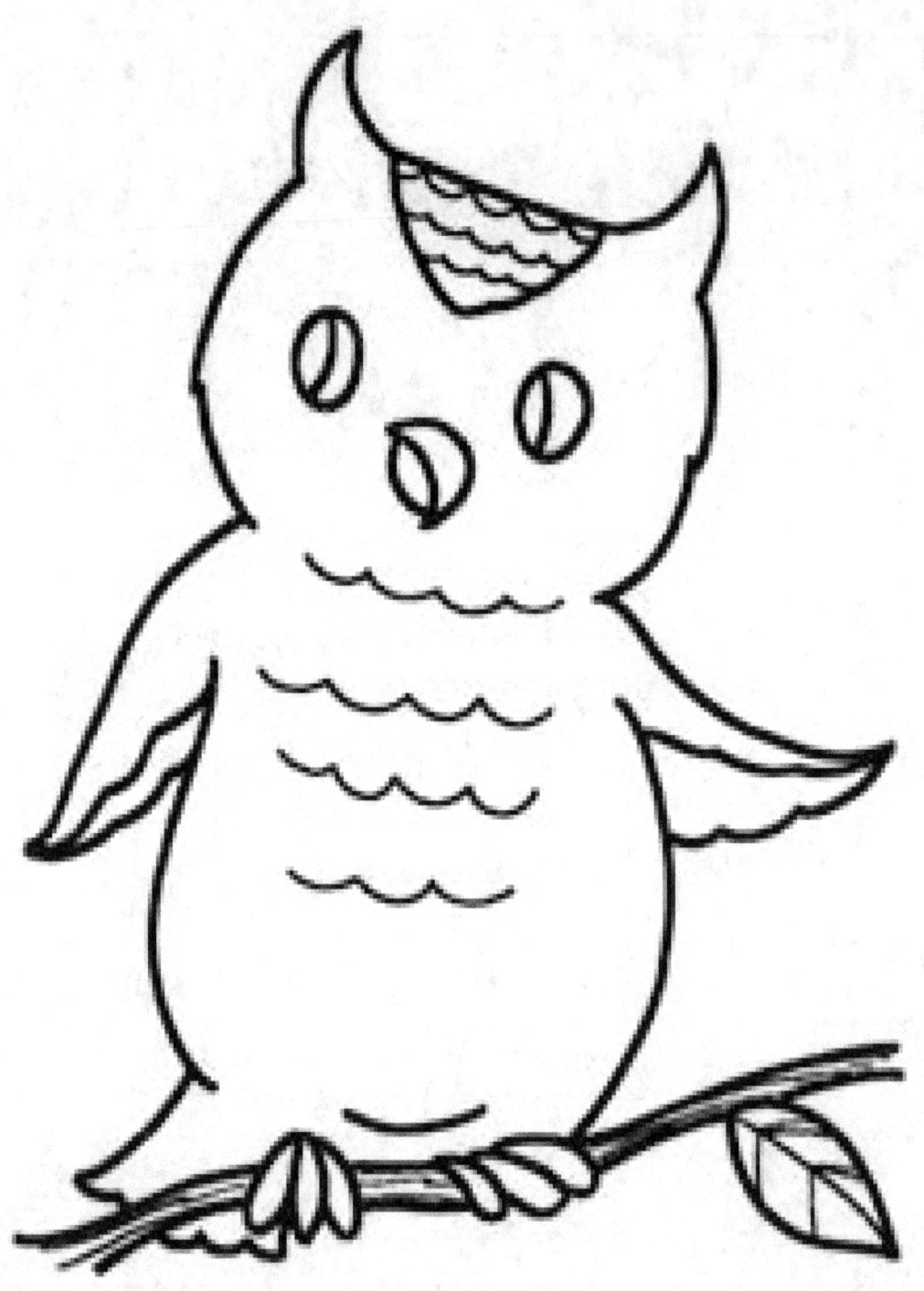

Mr. Owly Says, WHOO! WHOO!

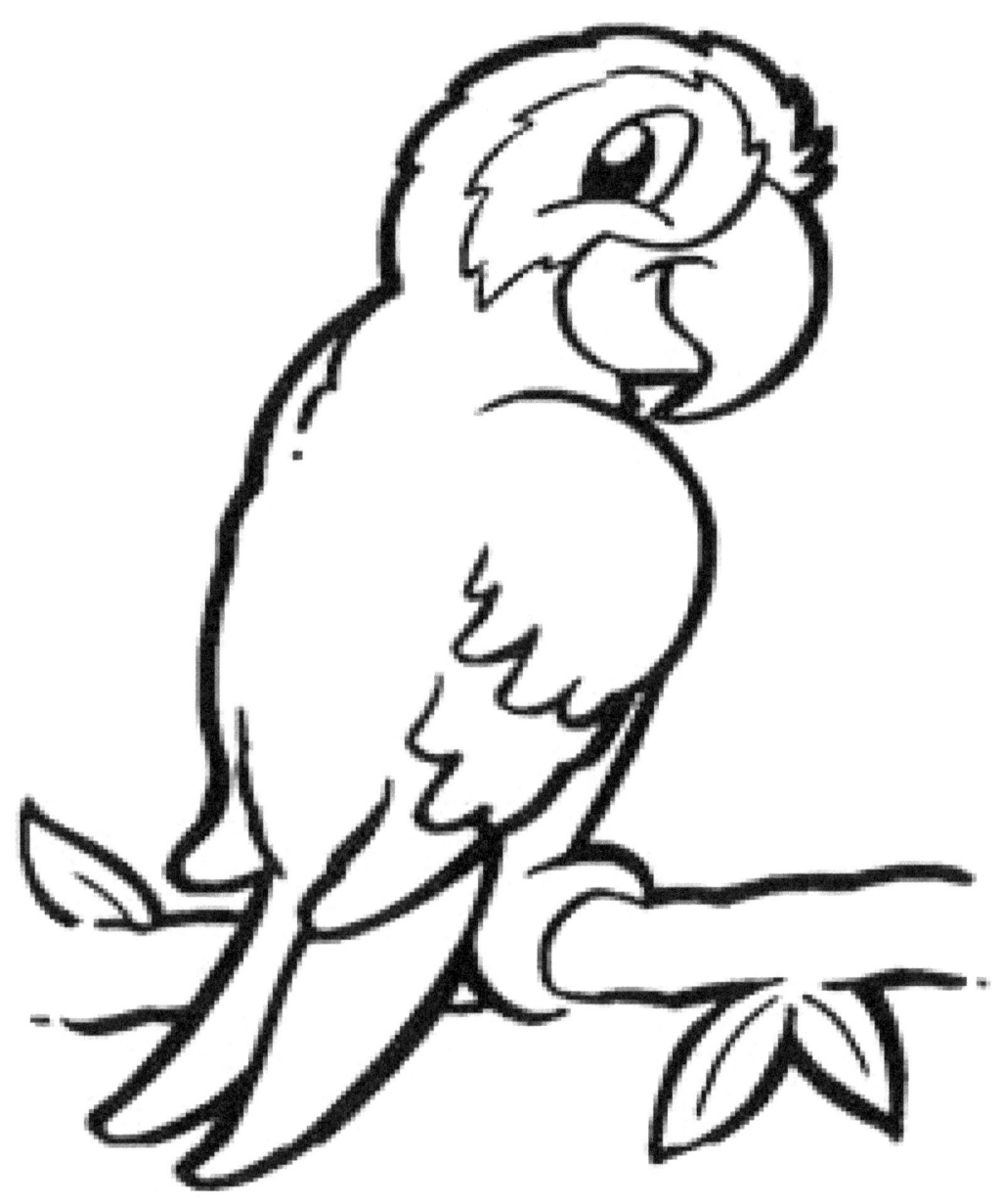

Use your Imagination and Color this little Fellow!

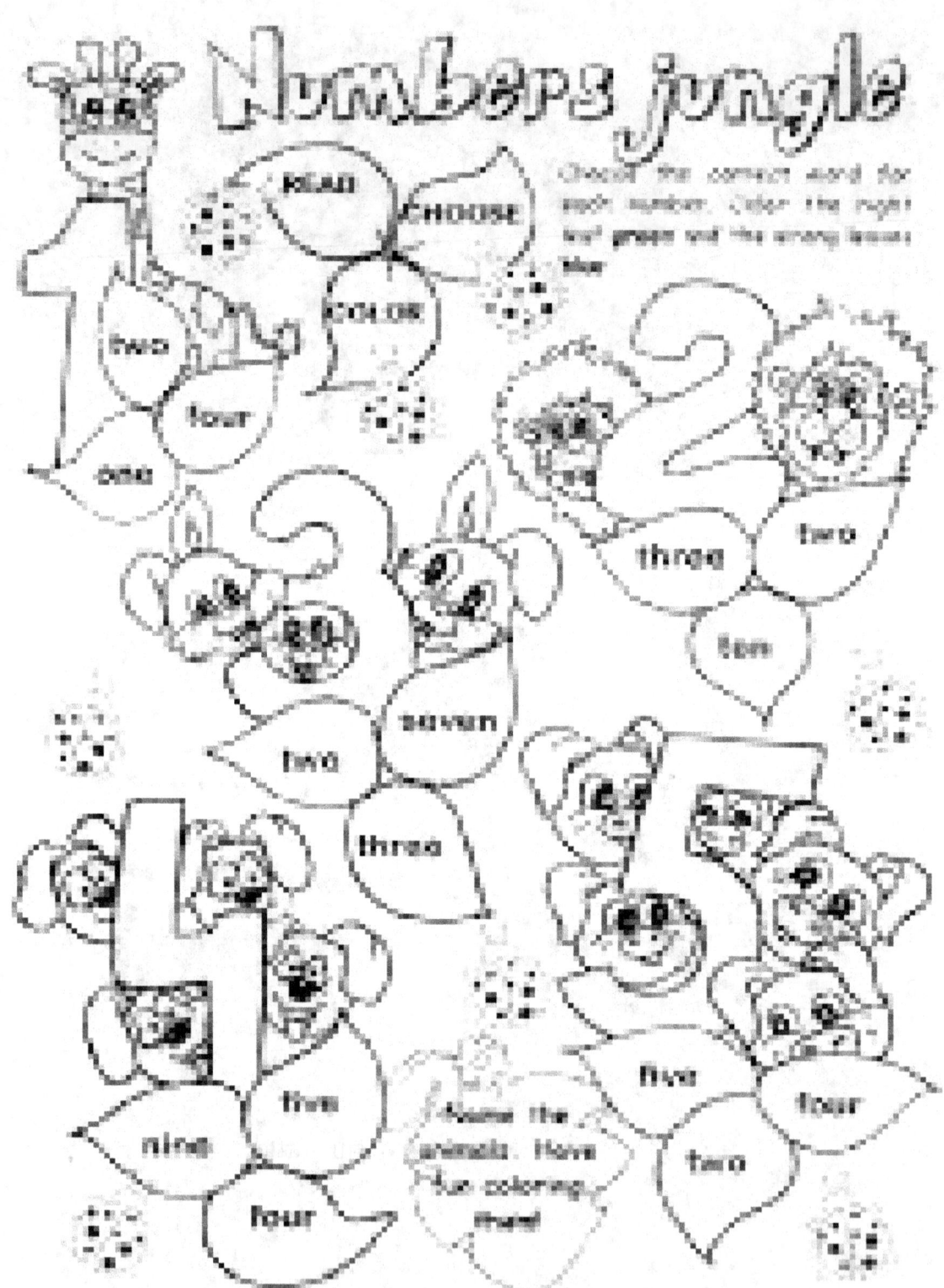

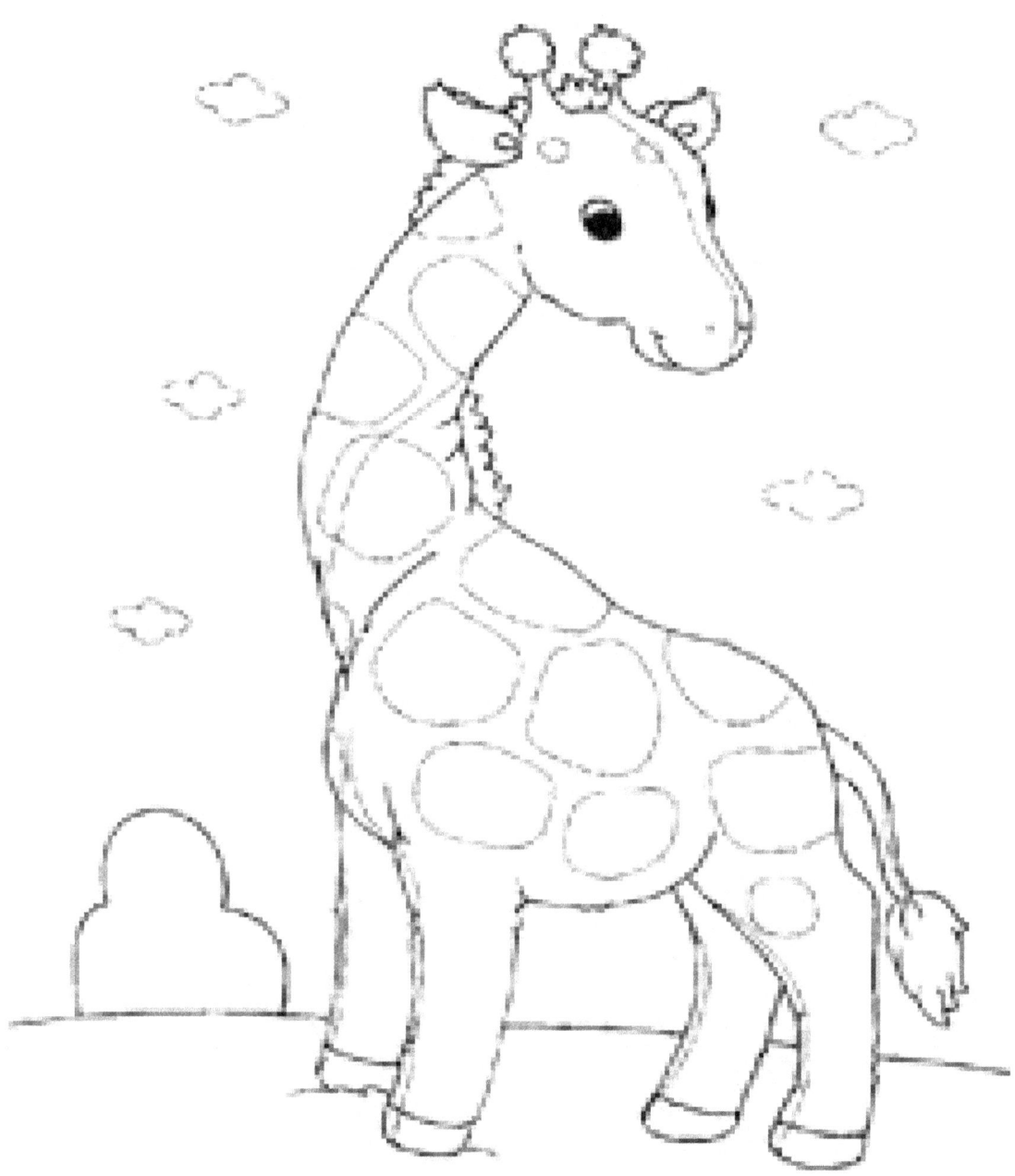

What animal am I ?

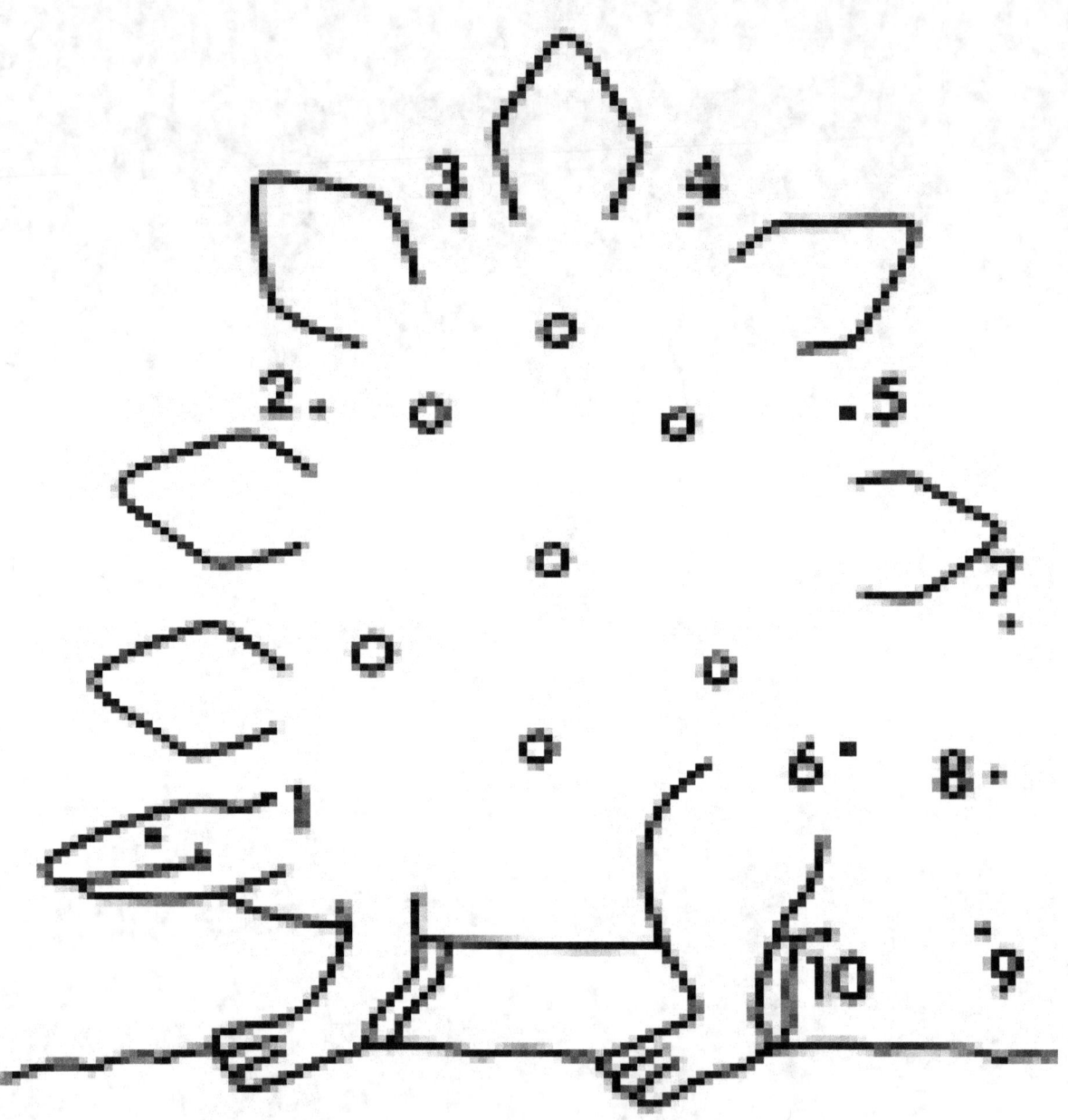

DO MY DOTS AND COLOR ME GREEN!

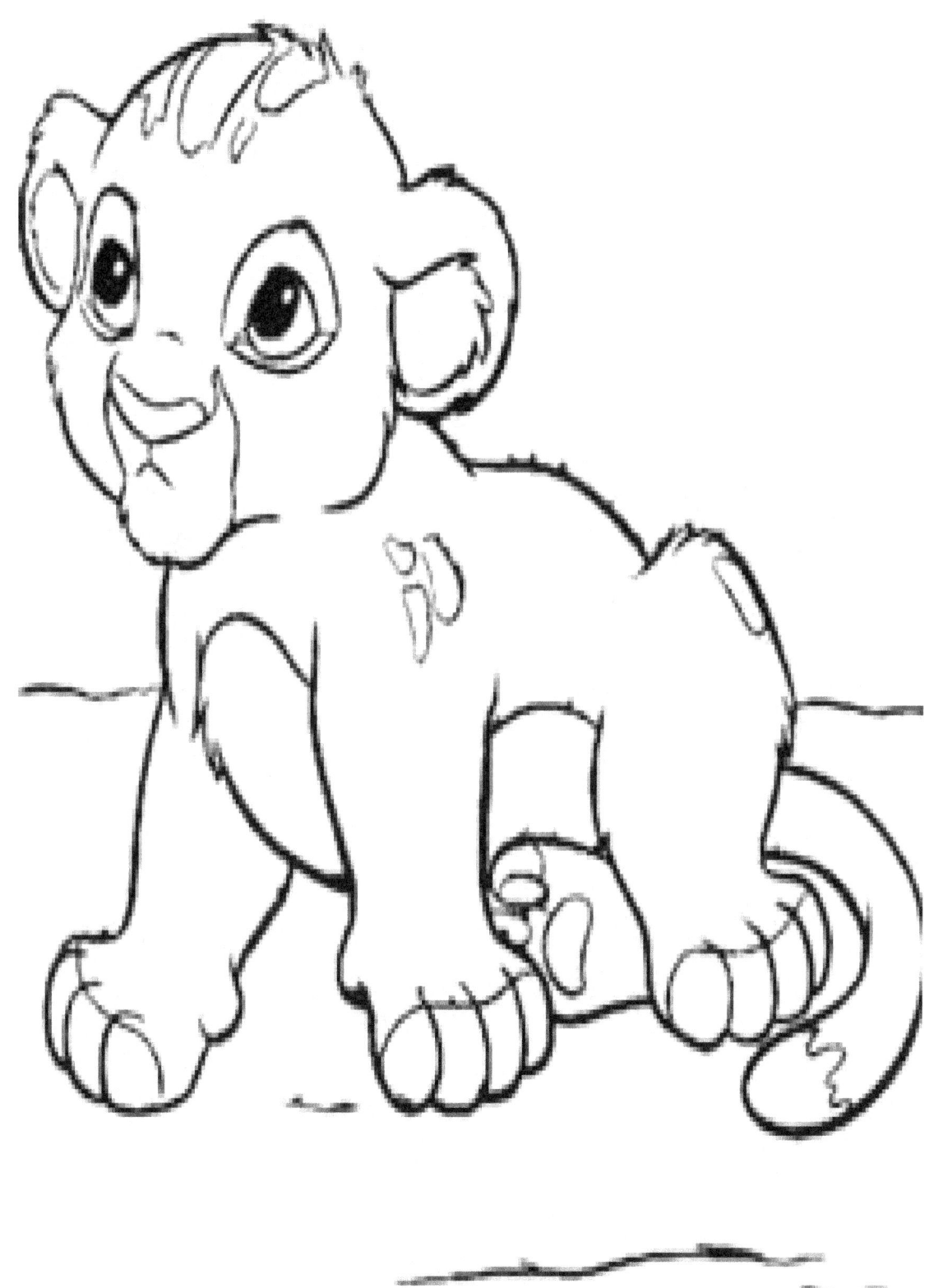

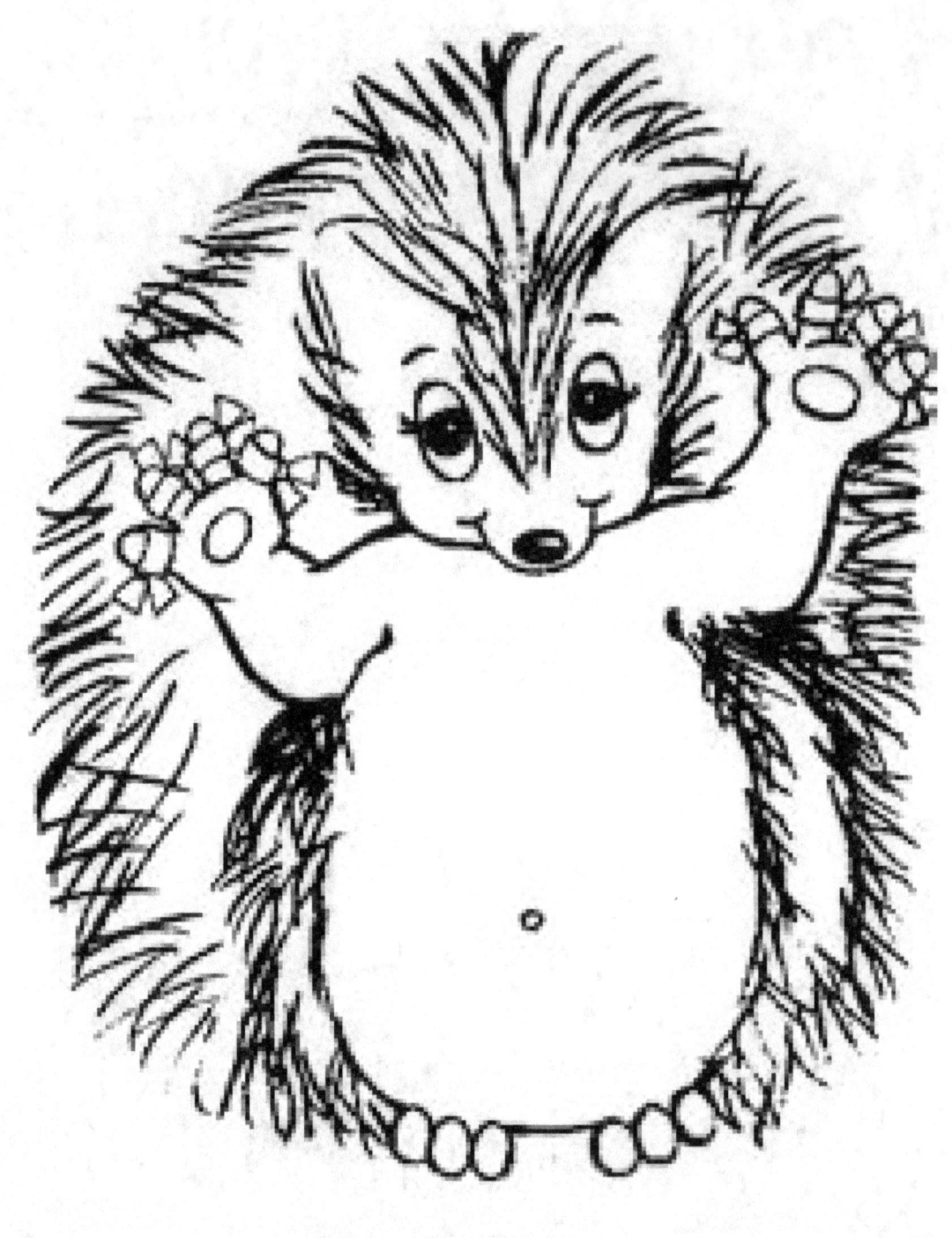

Hi my name is Prickles!!!!!

Do you know what I am?

ANIMALS

```
G E S U O M H N W R B W C W L
X D A Q H J X O O M L T H W J
B W S H N L H T P I C R A W M
Y W M E F F A R I G L K D O G
R C K R R R S Y K T H I P P O
J T O W I E F B X X L Q R J E
D R O T A G I L L A E B Z H X
T H N X P I C L F C R V Z S Z
V N H R S T H E T D R I B I Q
N Z A C S T Y X L W I N H F L
W U Q H K L J A E A U F A H F
V Q Q D P O Y K N V Q Z A T V
X M T L Q E T J Y E S Y R C H
T A C K Q C L K M O N K E Y R
P T S H W L Y E T D R A H T L
```

CAT	HIPPO	MOUSE	TIGER
DOG	SQUIRREL	MONKEY	
BIRD	GIRAFFE	ALLIGATOR	
ELEPHANT	FISH	LION	

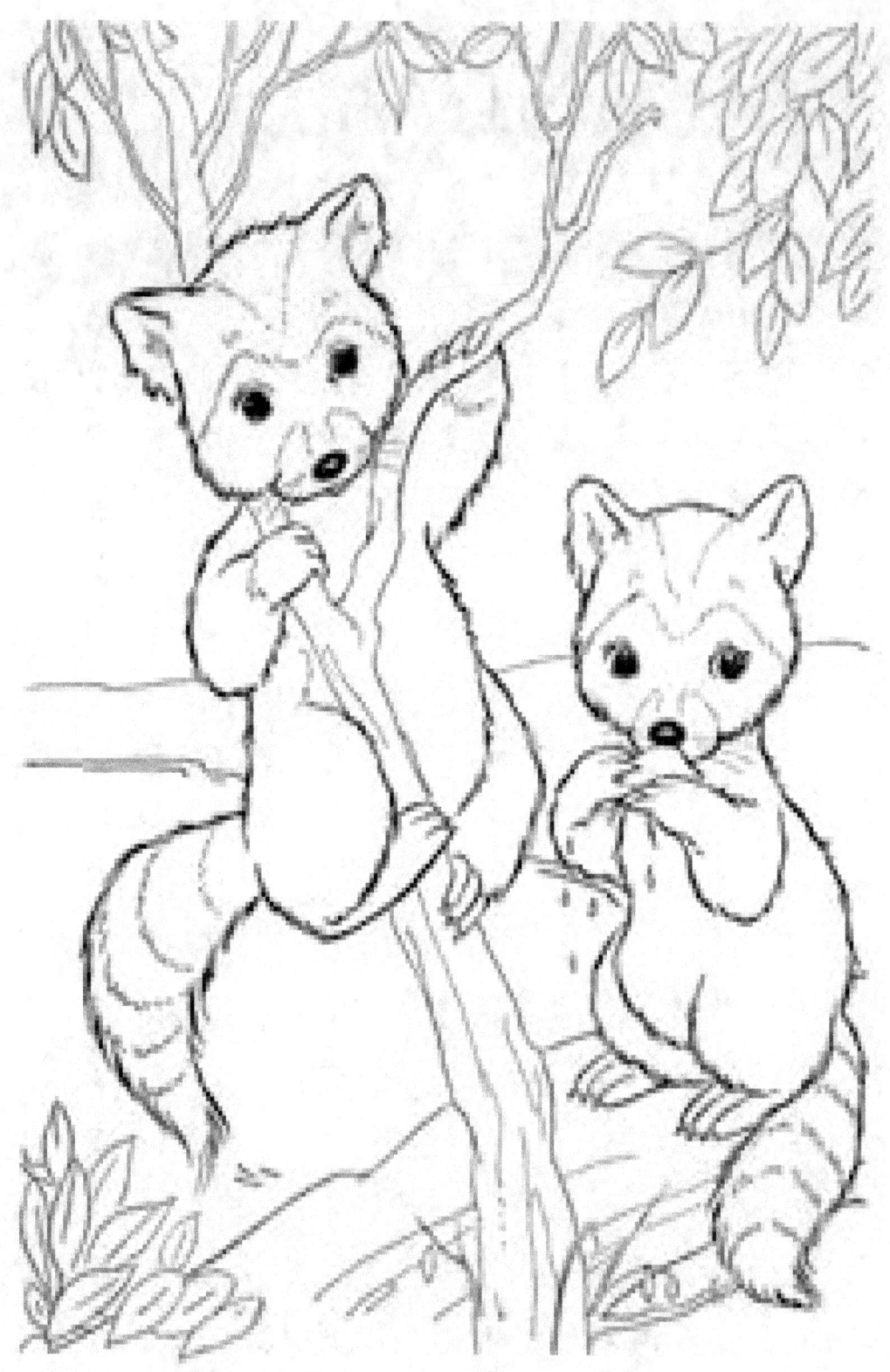

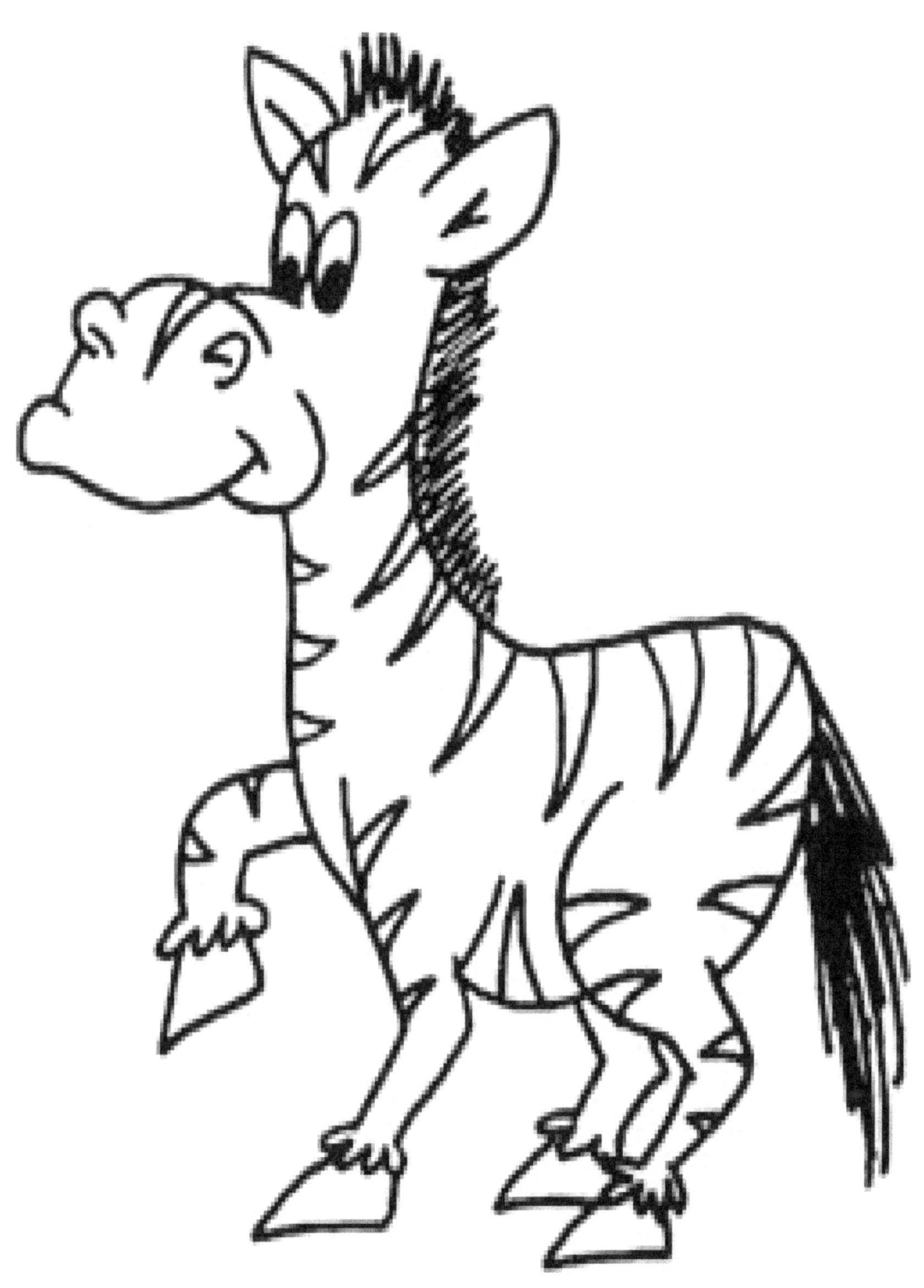

Mr. Stripey

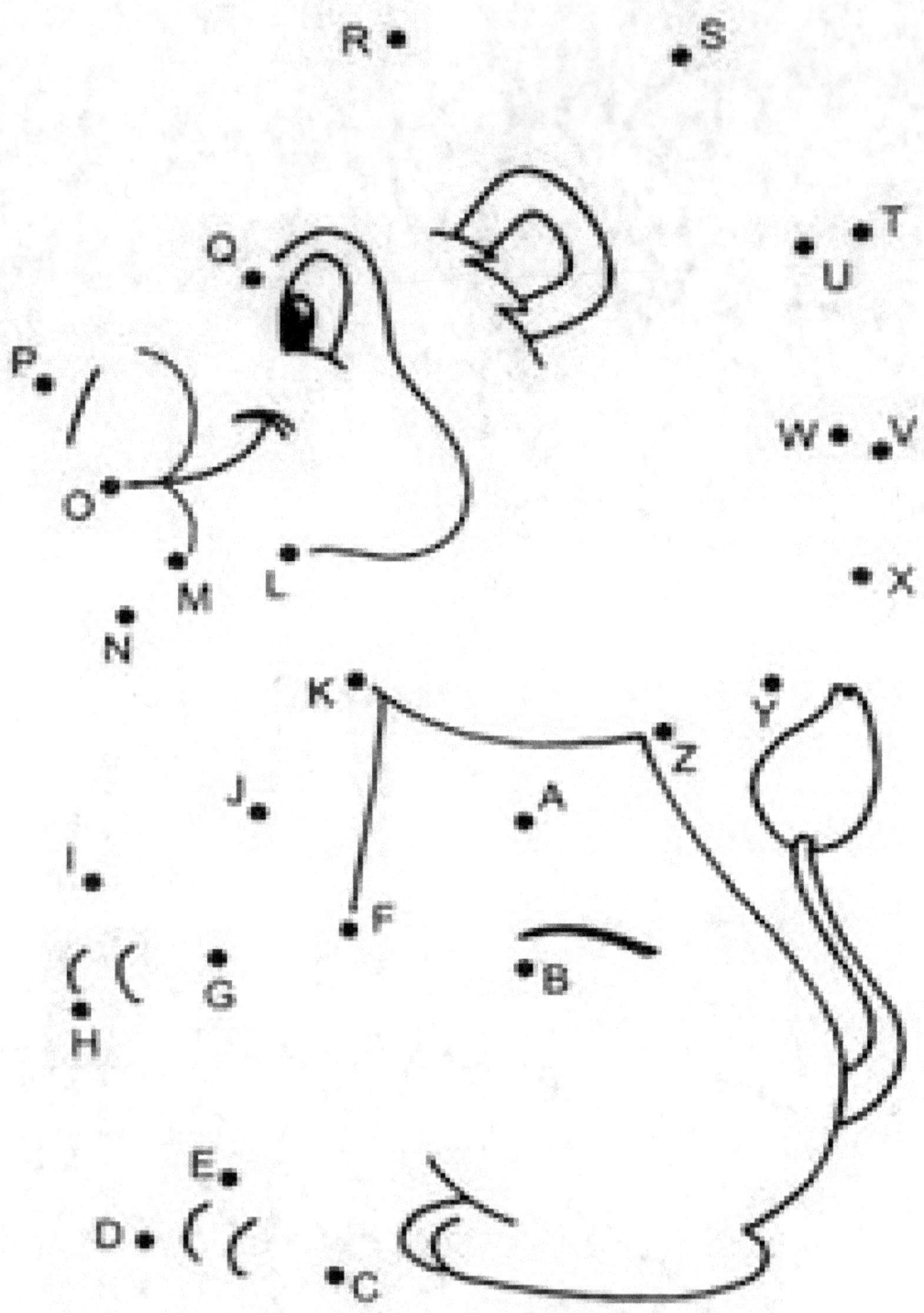

Enjoy this ABC Dot to Dot!

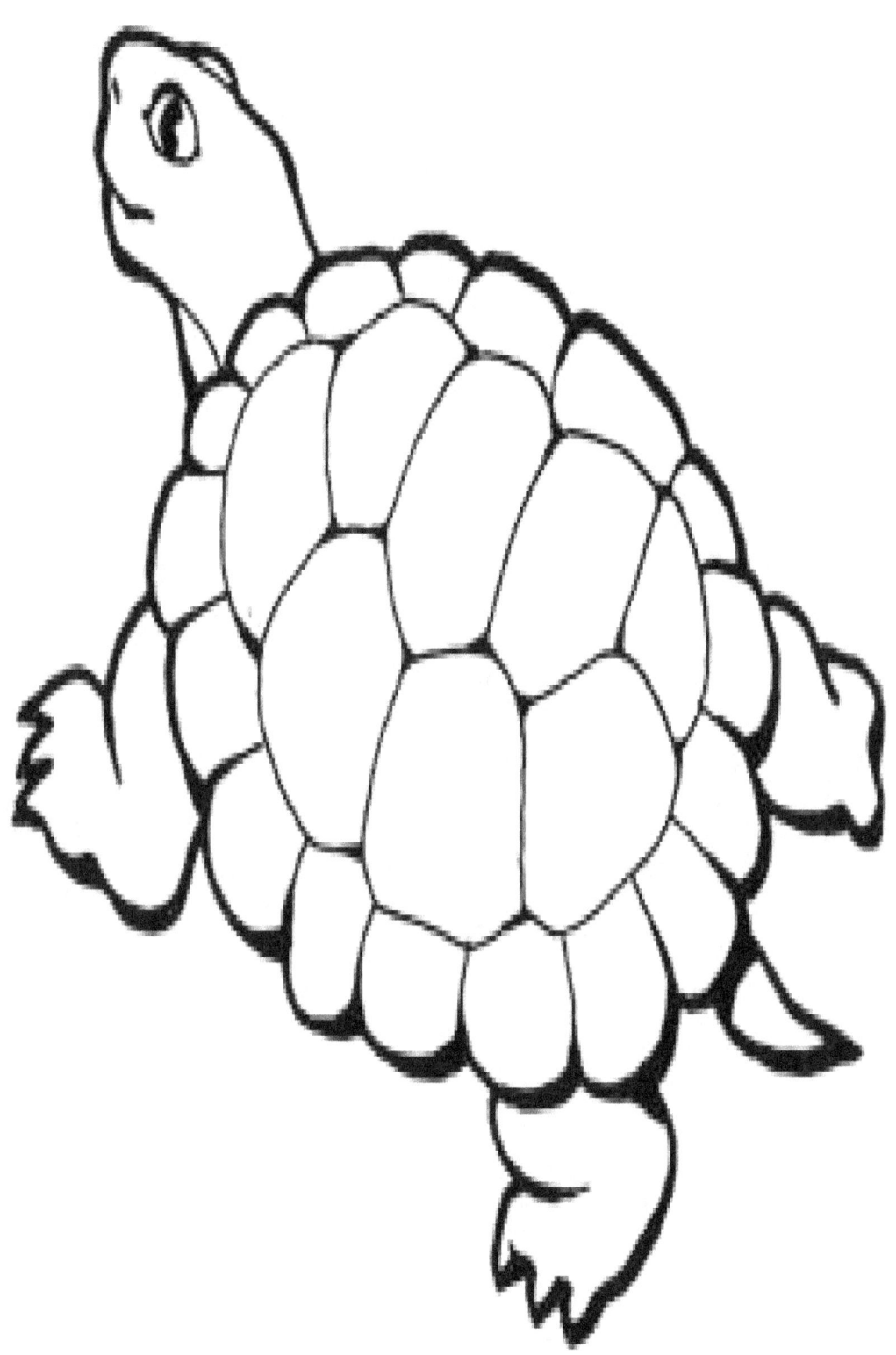

I might be slow but I can win the race!

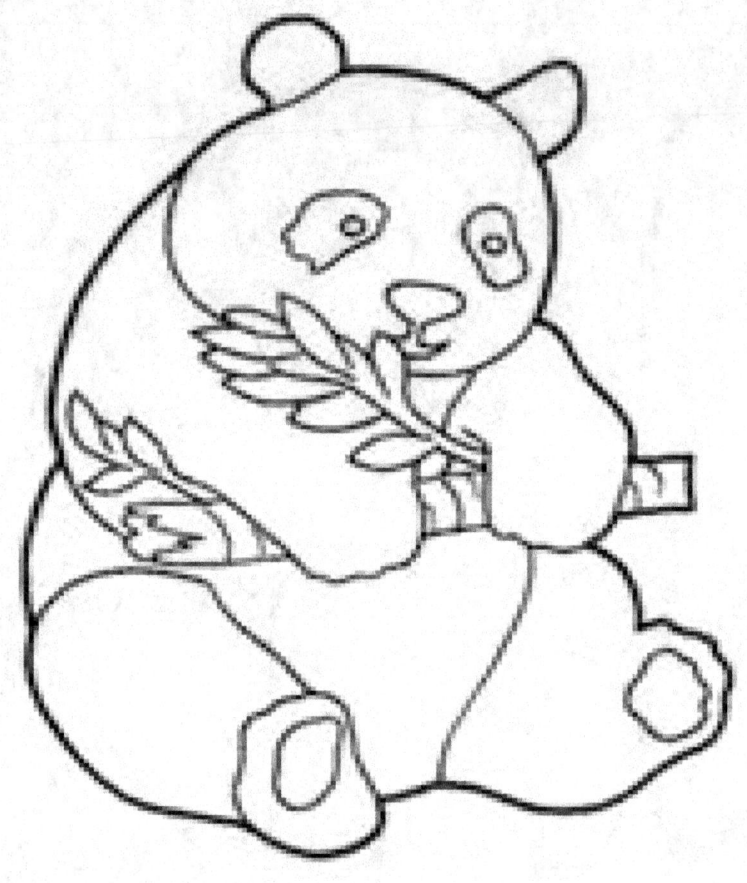

I'm a Panda What Colors Am I!

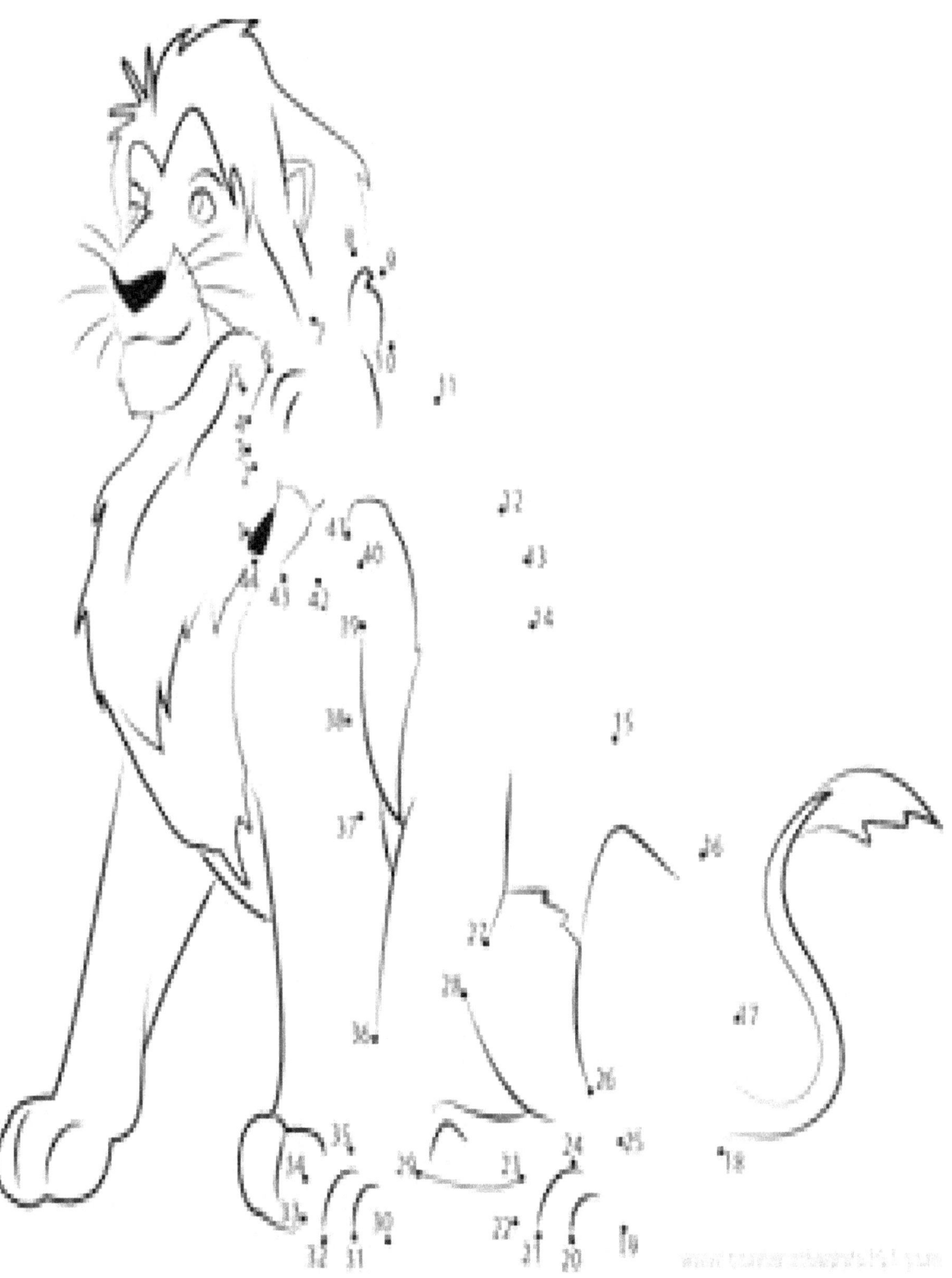

Animals Word Search

```
L K L N I W T C M L P K R E V
T N O B A E S R O H N G U W G
K V Q L L V F N C N I Z T B V
N B W I C W E P I Z J S A E C
T P M F X F B H S D P P B Q C
R O D J W U P U F J Y Q J X B
W L O R F O P A N D A L R S O
X B R G S K U N K N R E G I T
K Z T Y M X O D H G K L B R T
P I G S N A K E D B W O C G C
A R K C M Y M Q X O V V A E Q
S B E A R S Q H S E A L E A A
D O G R A B B I T I H Q P K B
J N O I L X E O C A T U G Q V
V L A R B E Z O C R E P A I C
```

APE	HORSE	SEAL
BEAR	LION	SKUNK
CAT	PANDA	SNAKE
COW	PIG	TIGER
DOG	RABBIT	ZEBRA

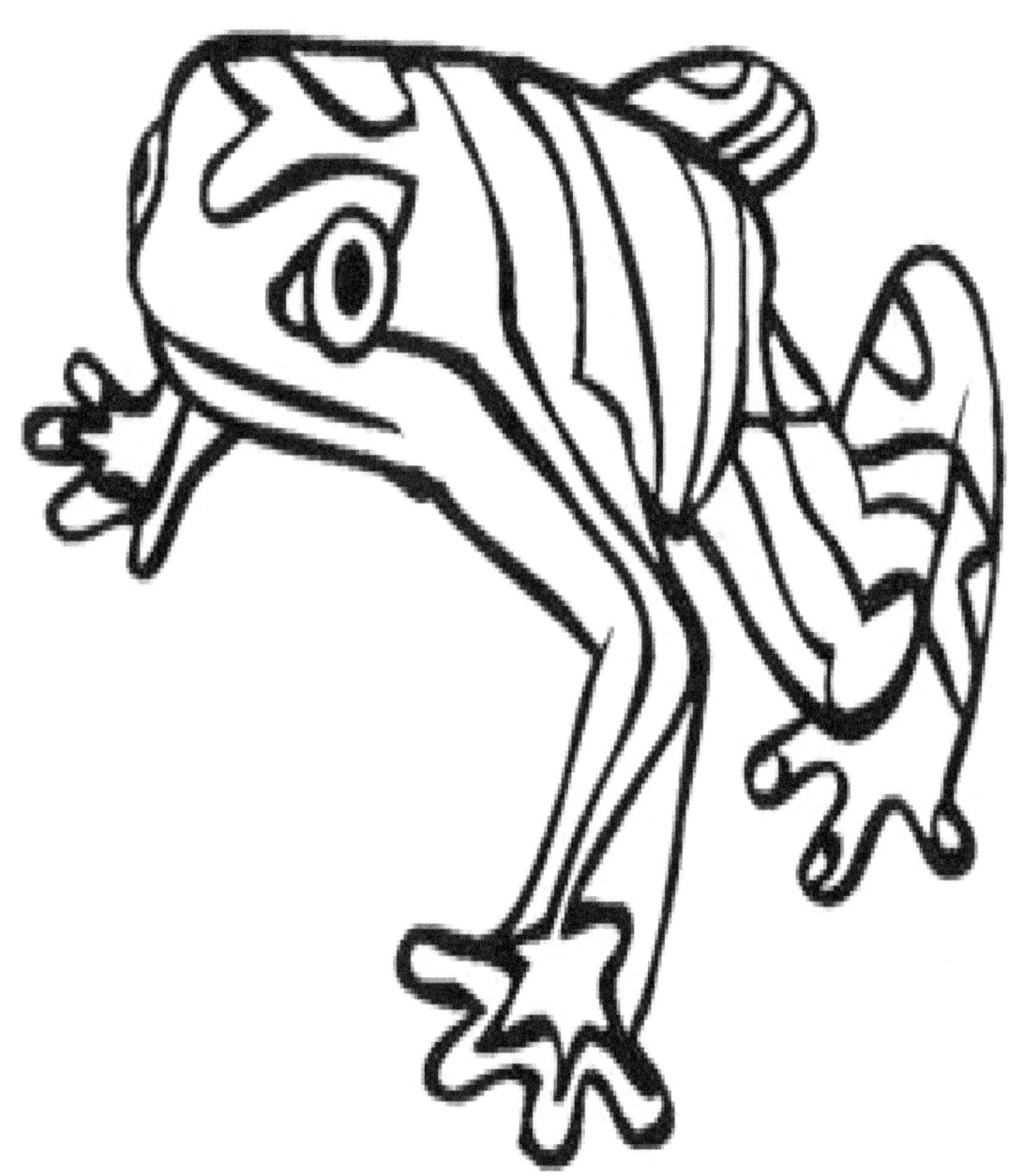

Animal Kingdom
Word Search

```
b e a r s r a
i l i o n a l
r e s w a b l
d p w l k b i
w h a l e t a
p a n d a t a
i n t o a d t
g t i g e r o
z e b r a x r
```

Bear
Lion
Elephant
Whale
Panda
Pig
Ant (x 2)
Kitty
Owl
Rabbit
Snake
Bird
Dog
Toad
Swan
Alligator
Zebra

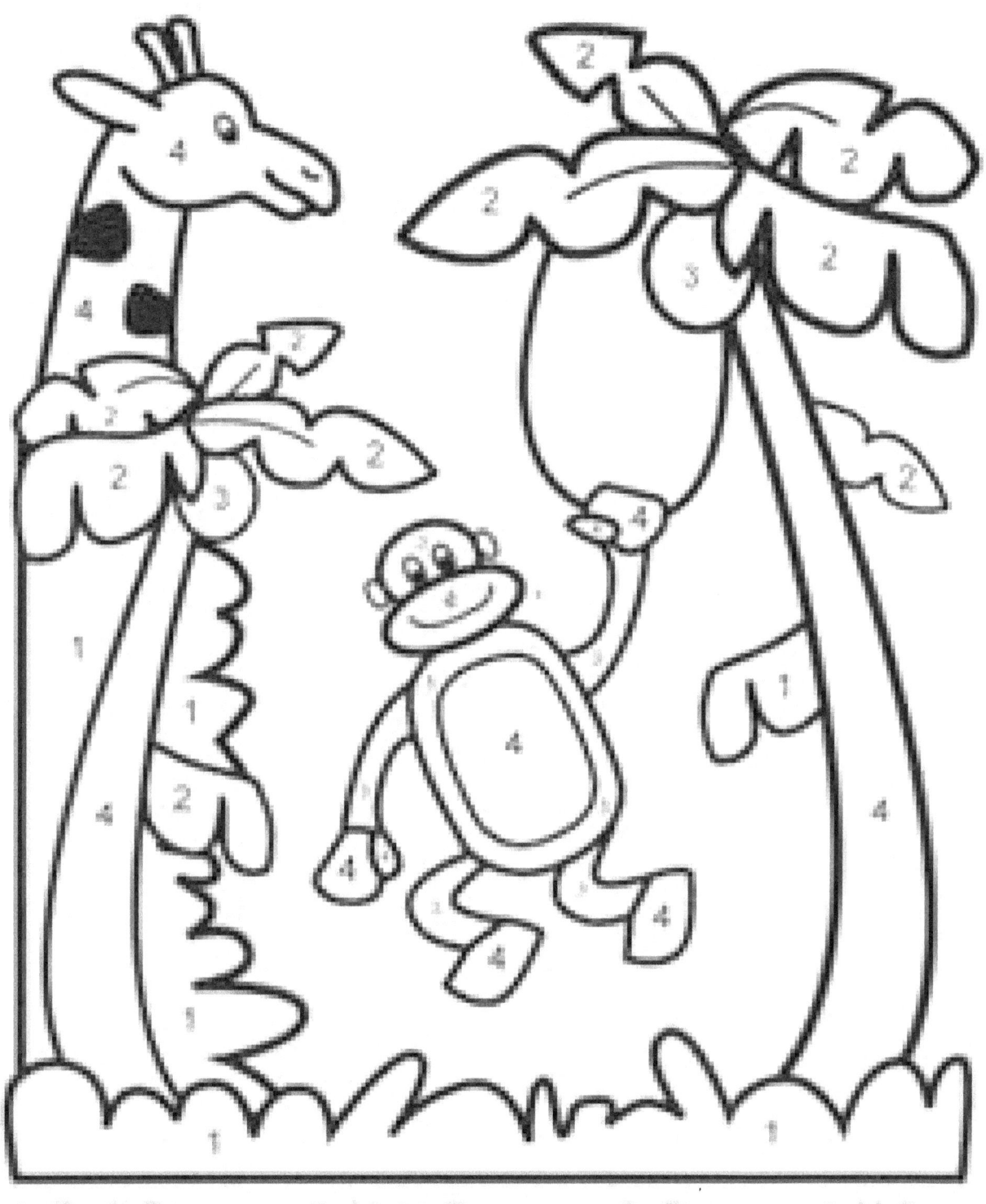

1=Dark Green   2=Light Green   3=Brown   4=Yellow

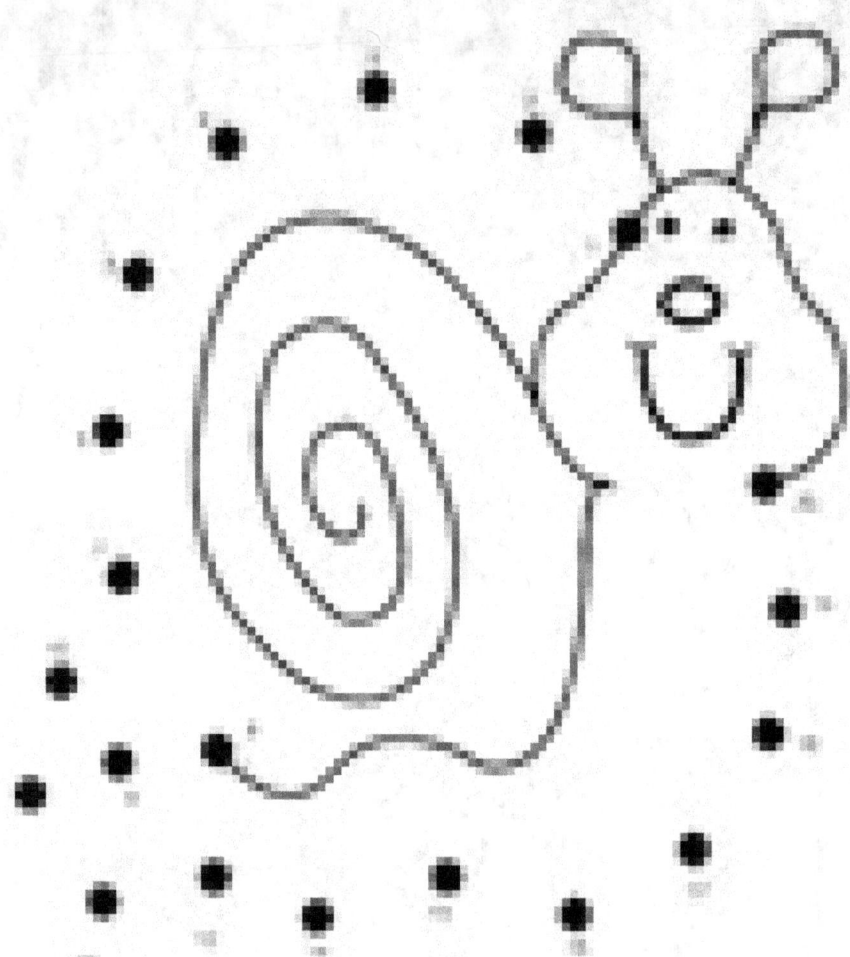

Do the Dot to Dot and use your imagination to color me!

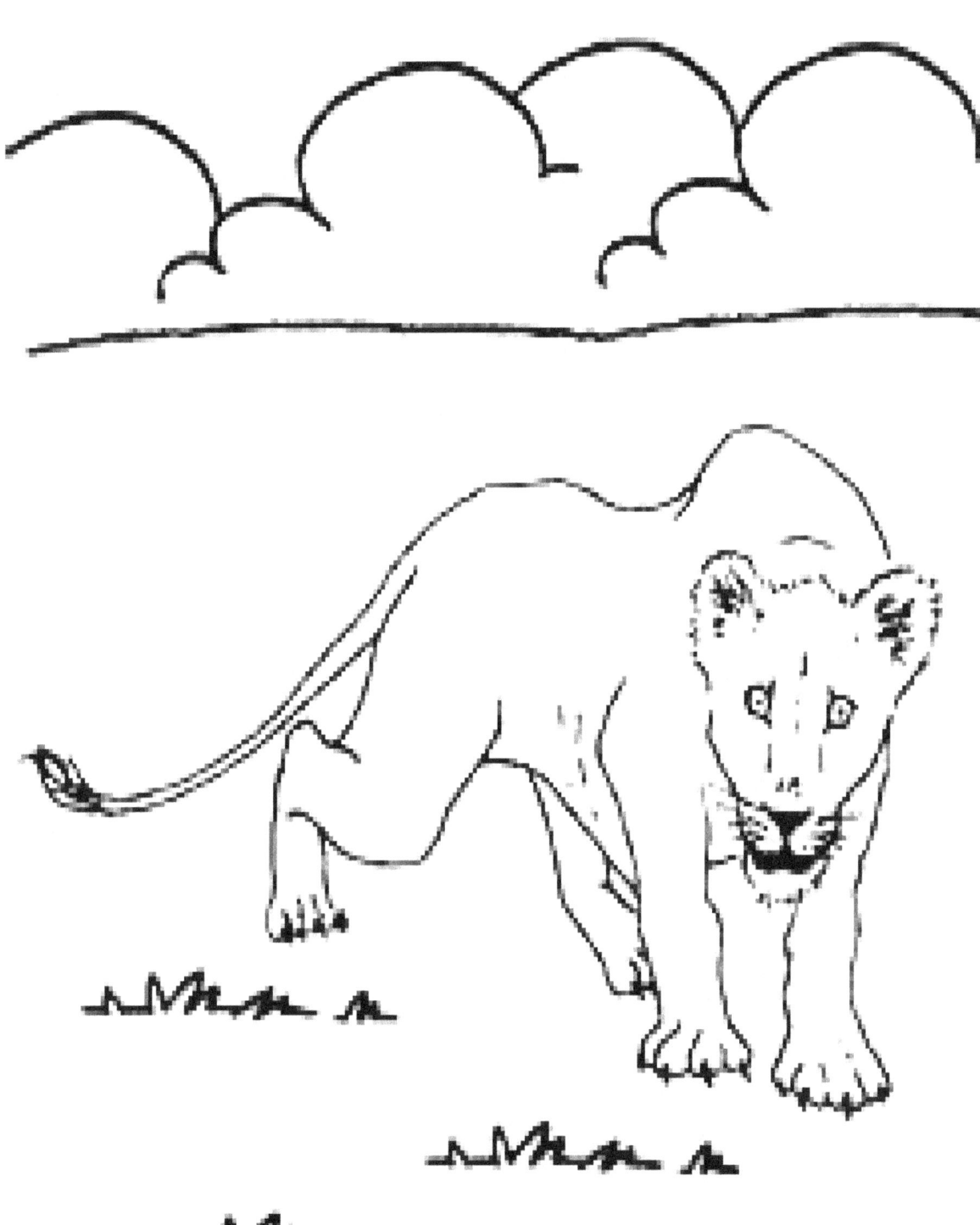

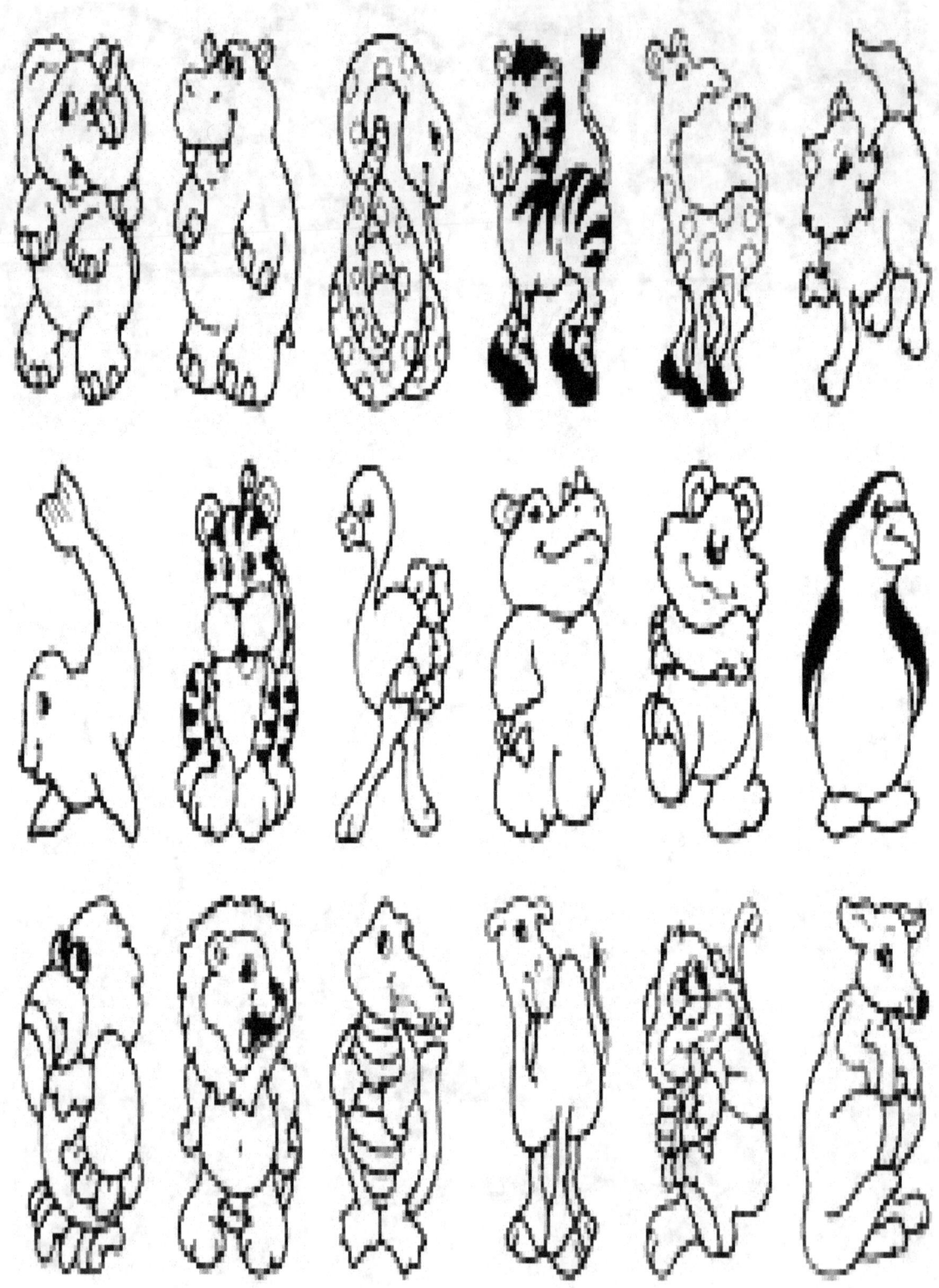

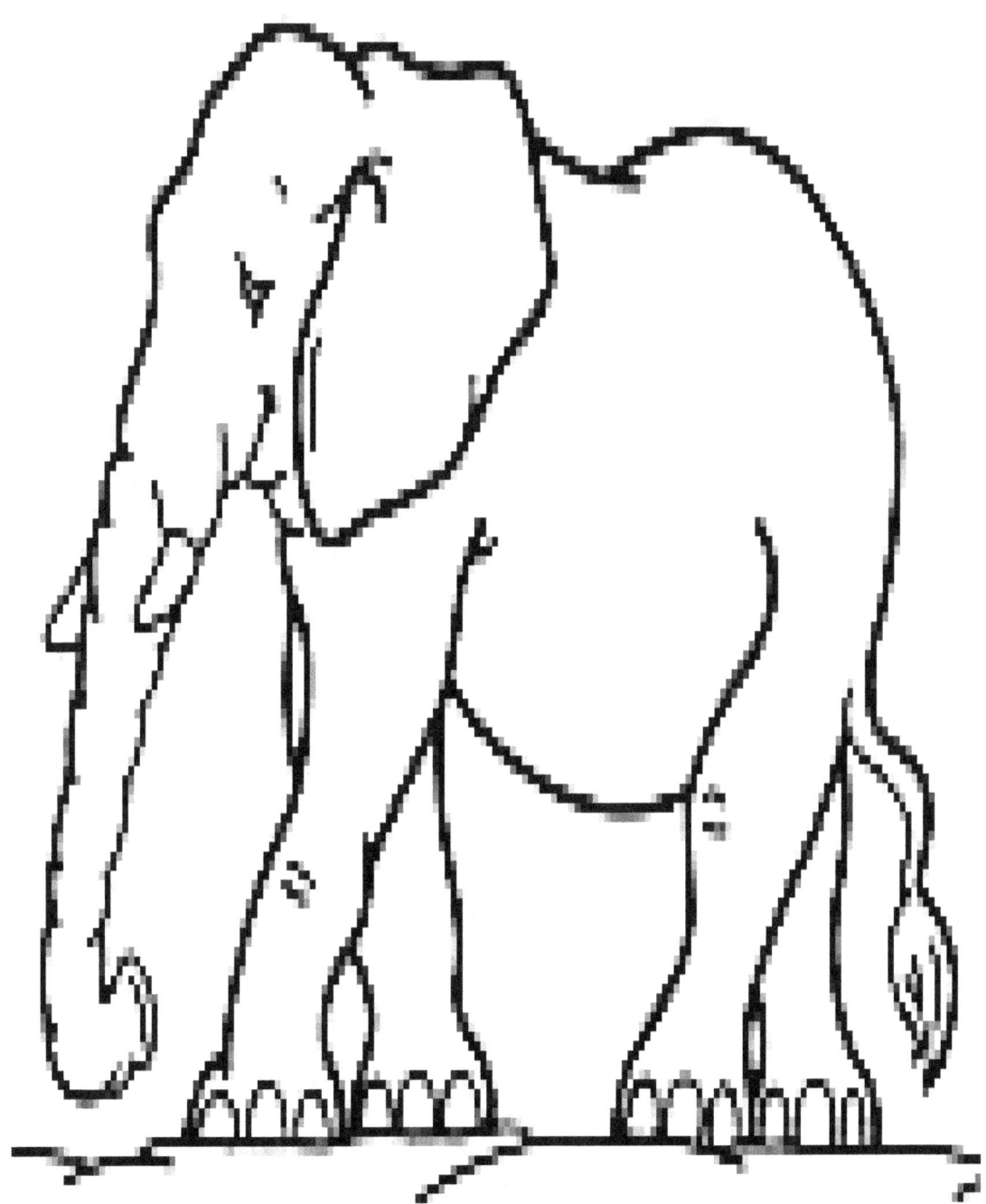

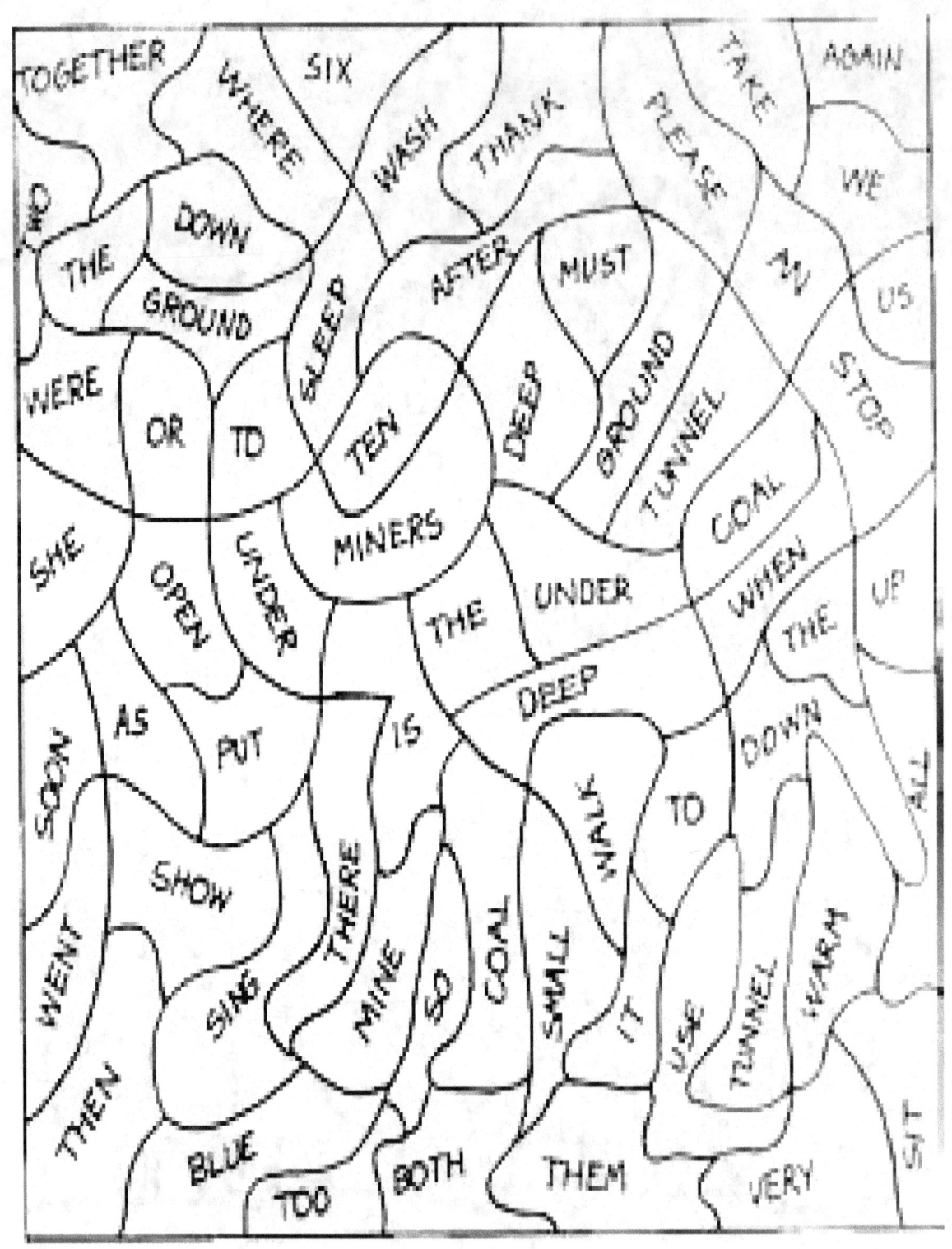

Color all Colors!

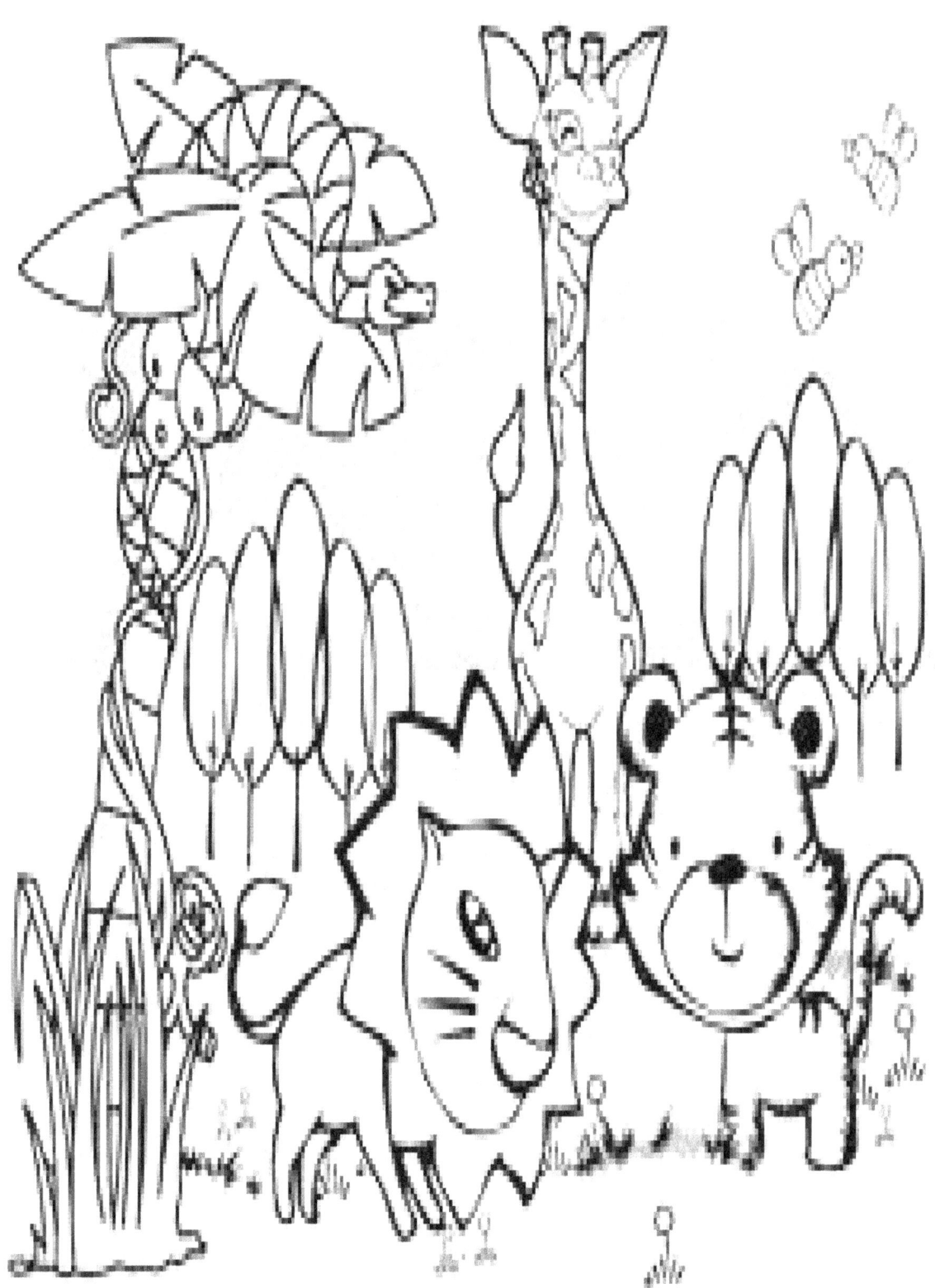

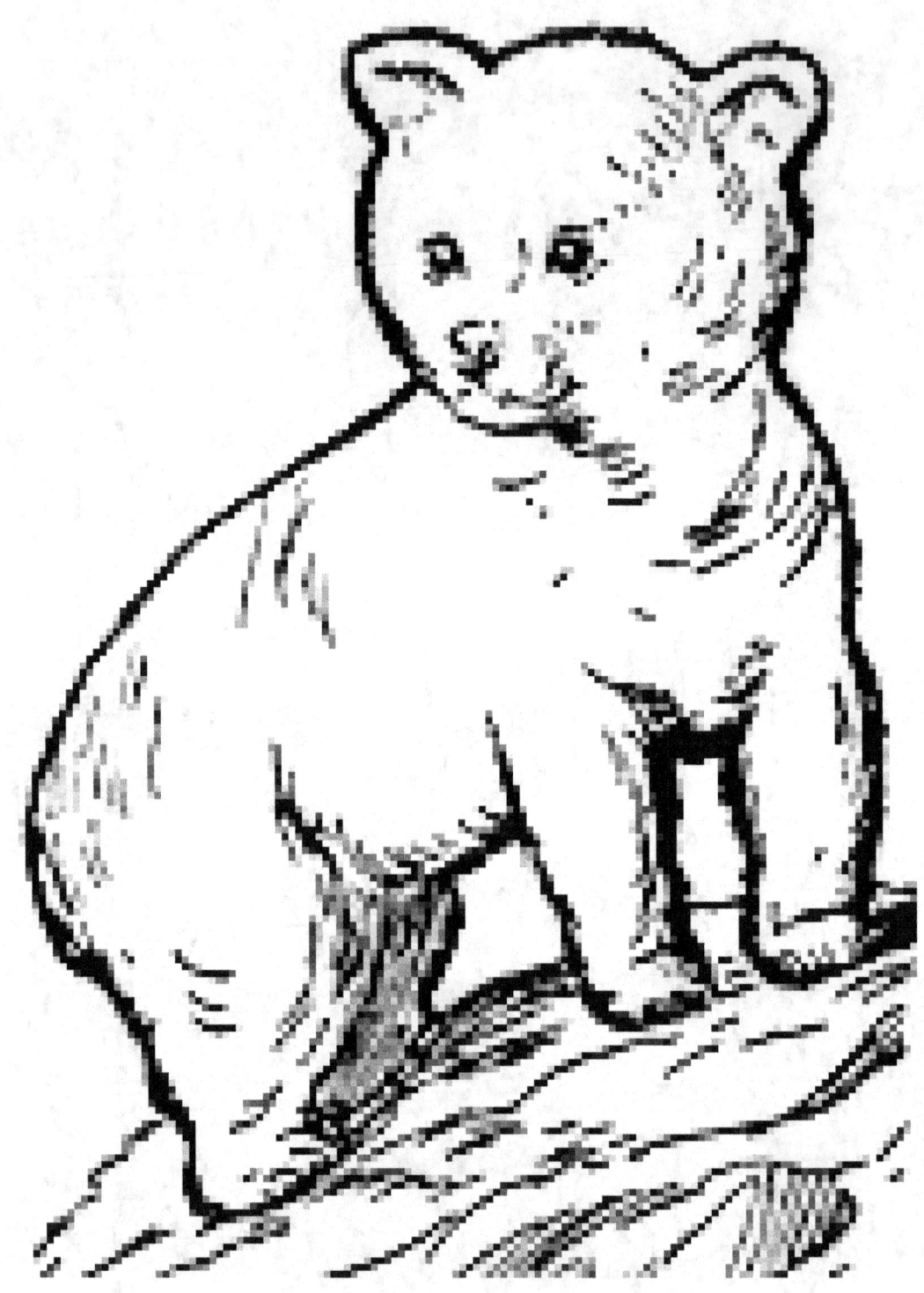

Little Henry Loves to Climb!

Take this Page Write your ABC's

See How Many Numbers you can Write on this page!

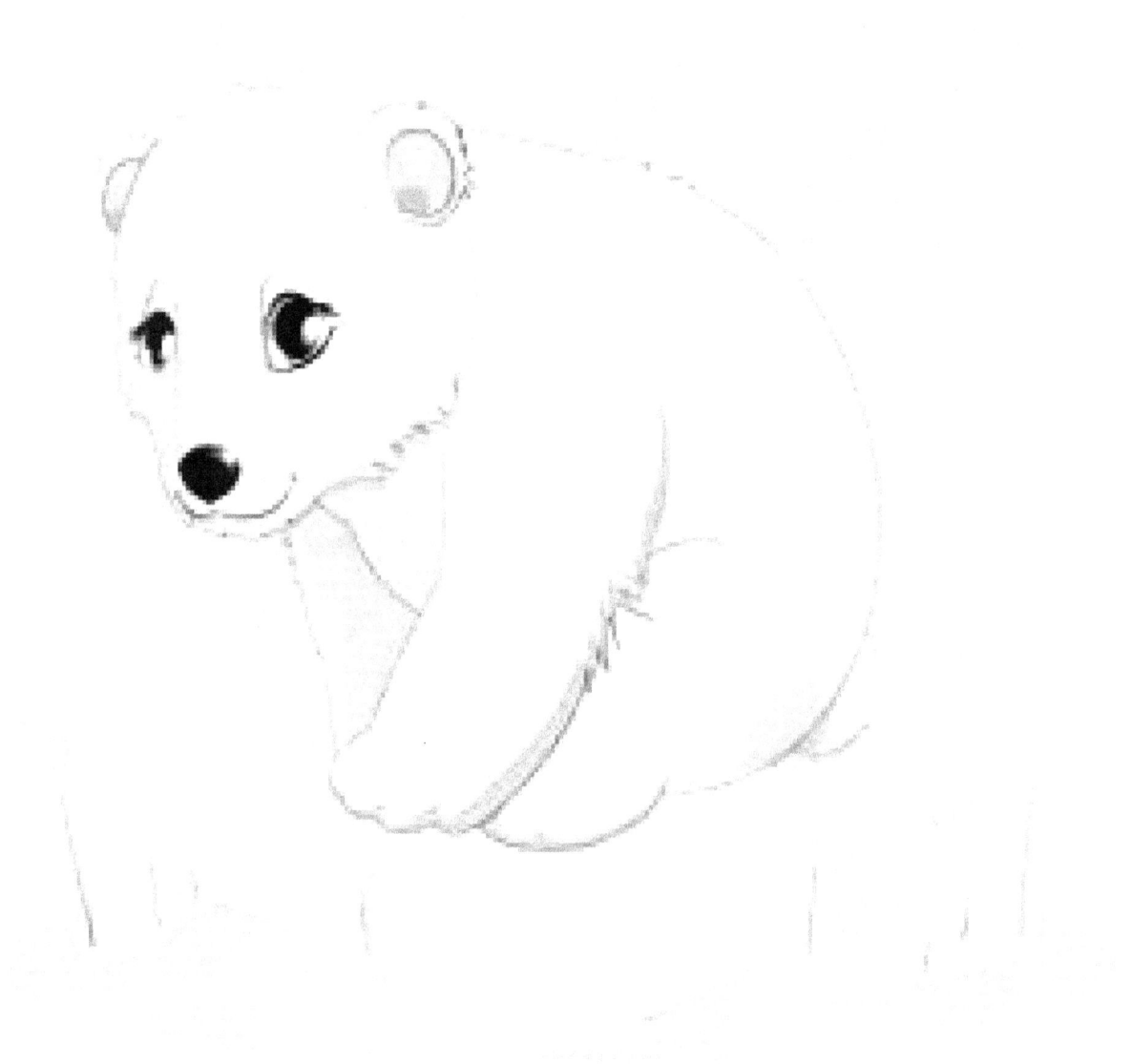

What Kind of Bear Is This?

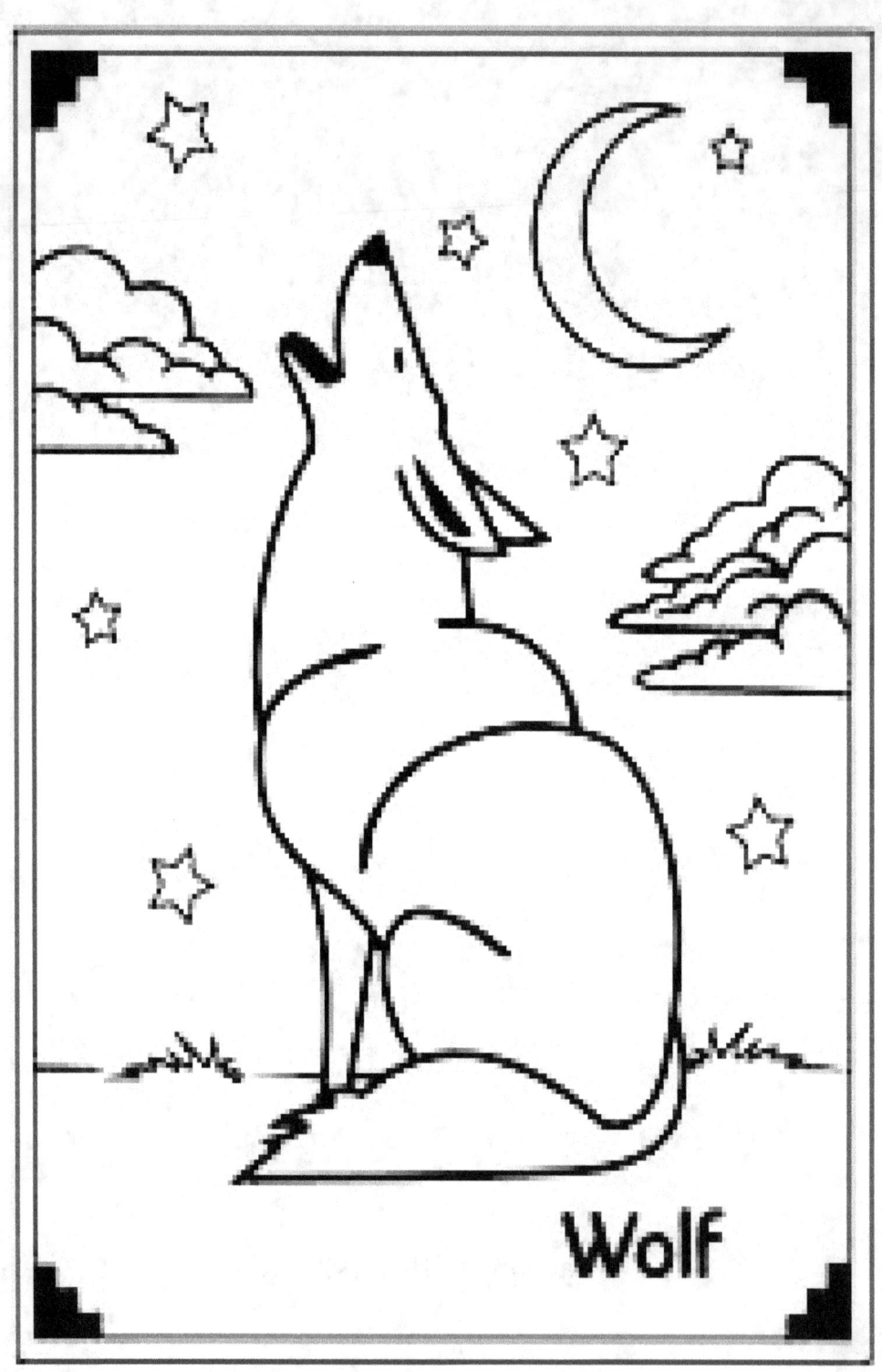

Wolf

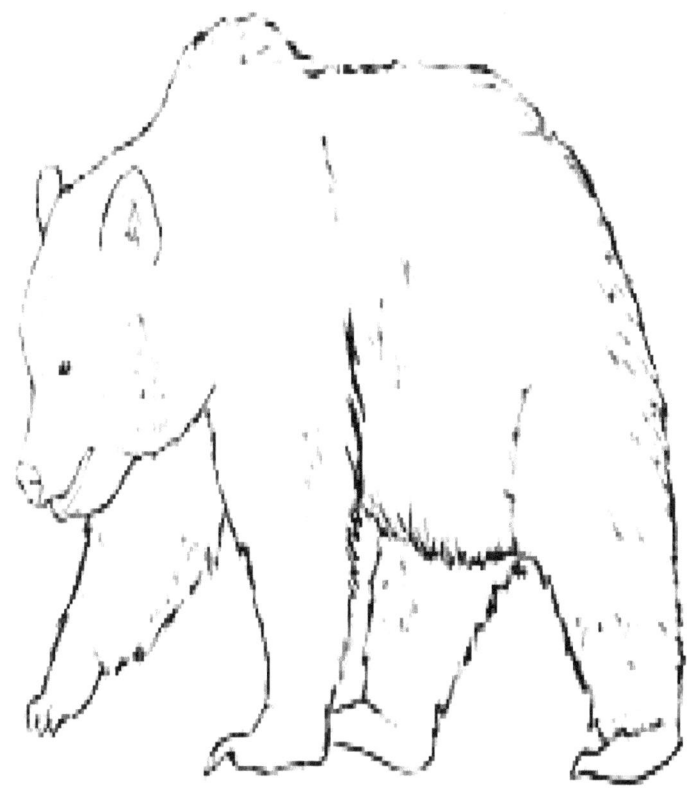

Can you draw this hungry Bear some Honey?

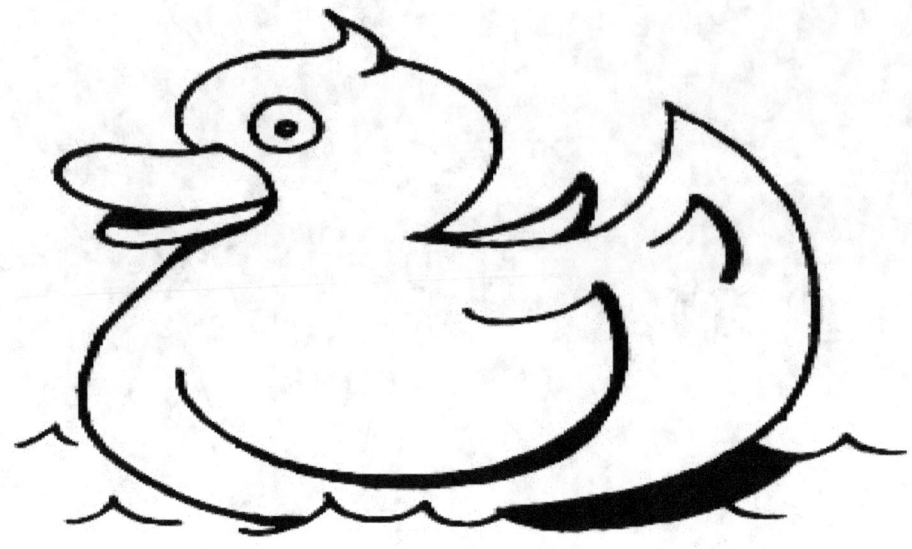

Color The Duck Yellow, then make him some extra water to float on!

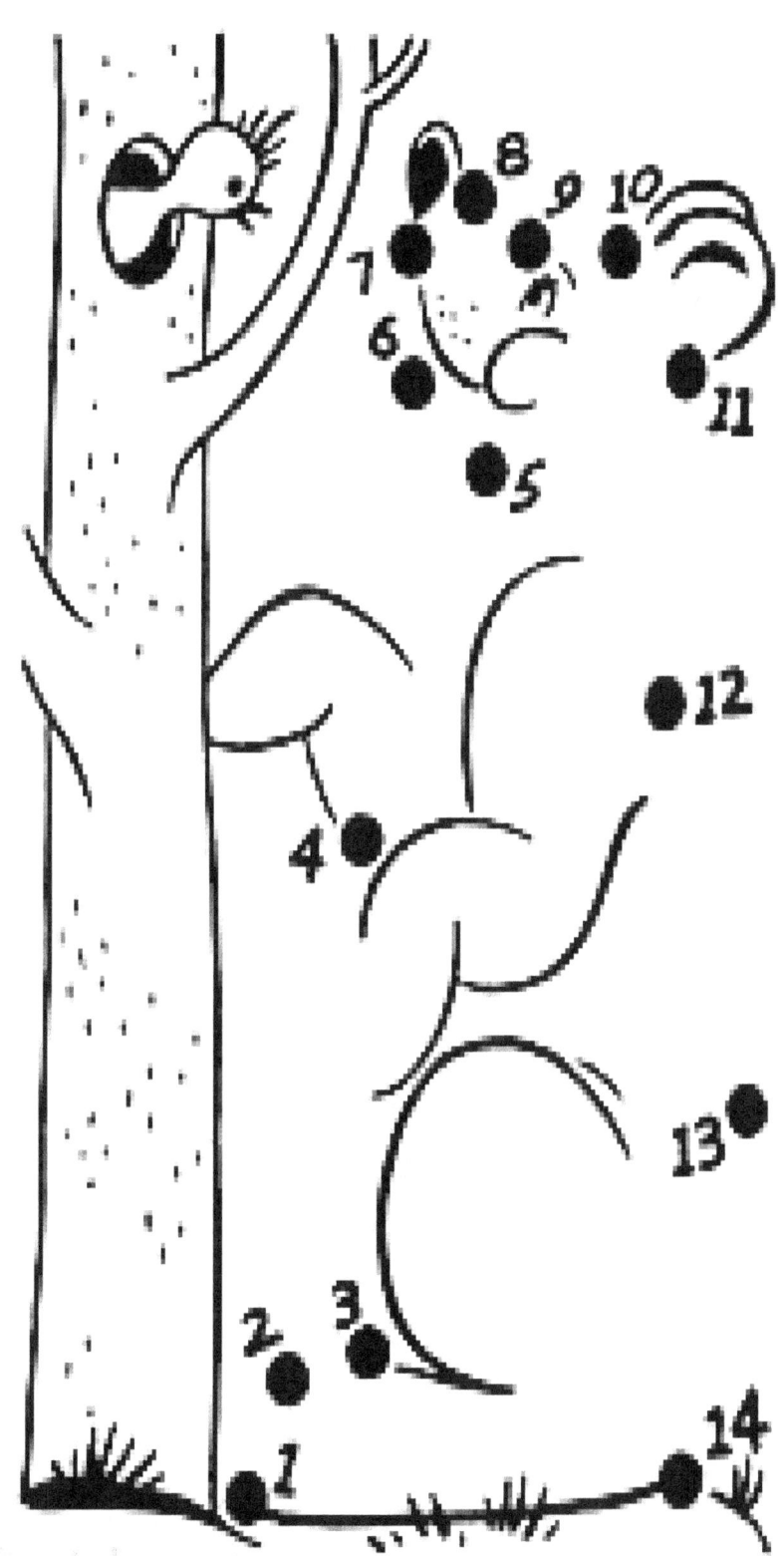

Draw Your Favorite Wild Animal HERE!

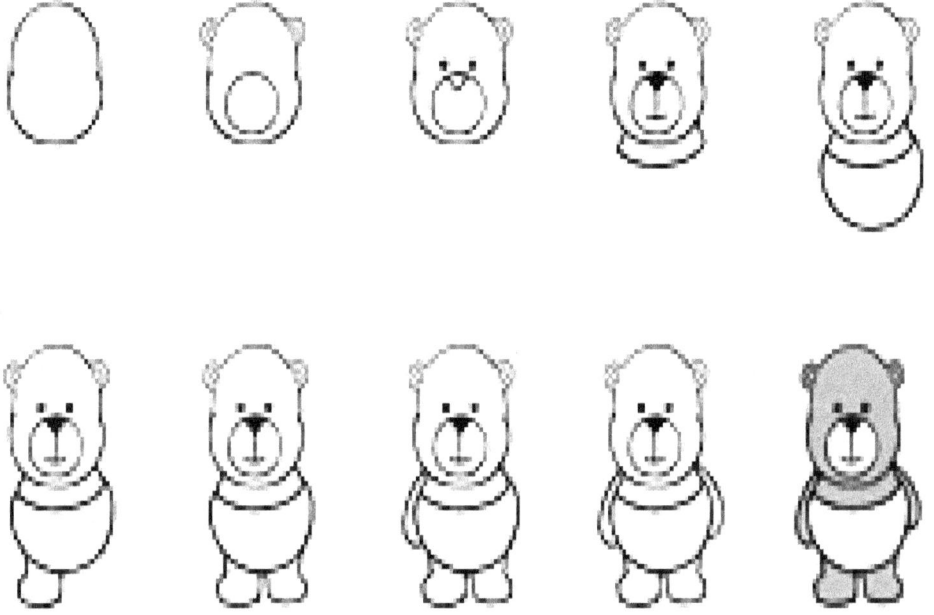

See If you can draw this cutie!

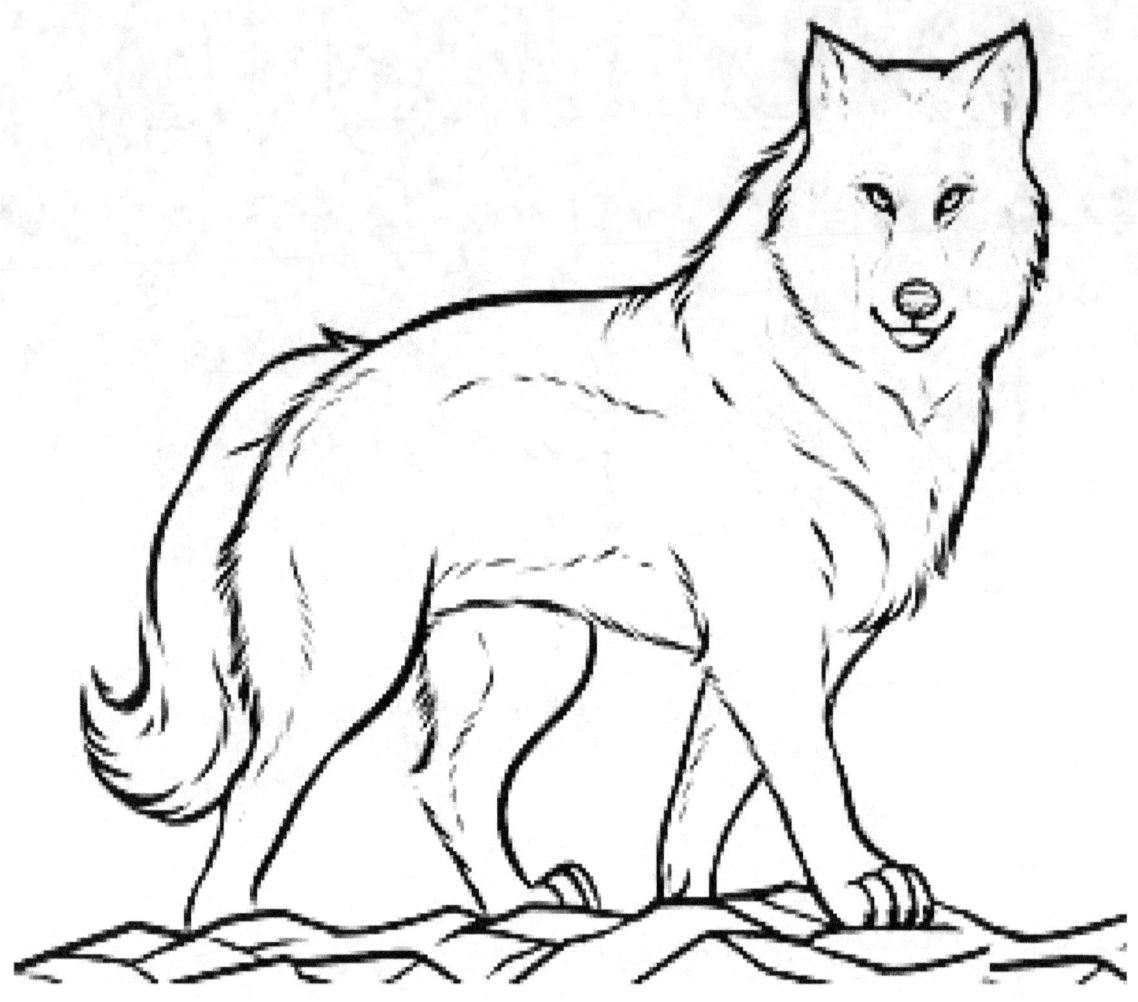

What is this fine looking Creature?

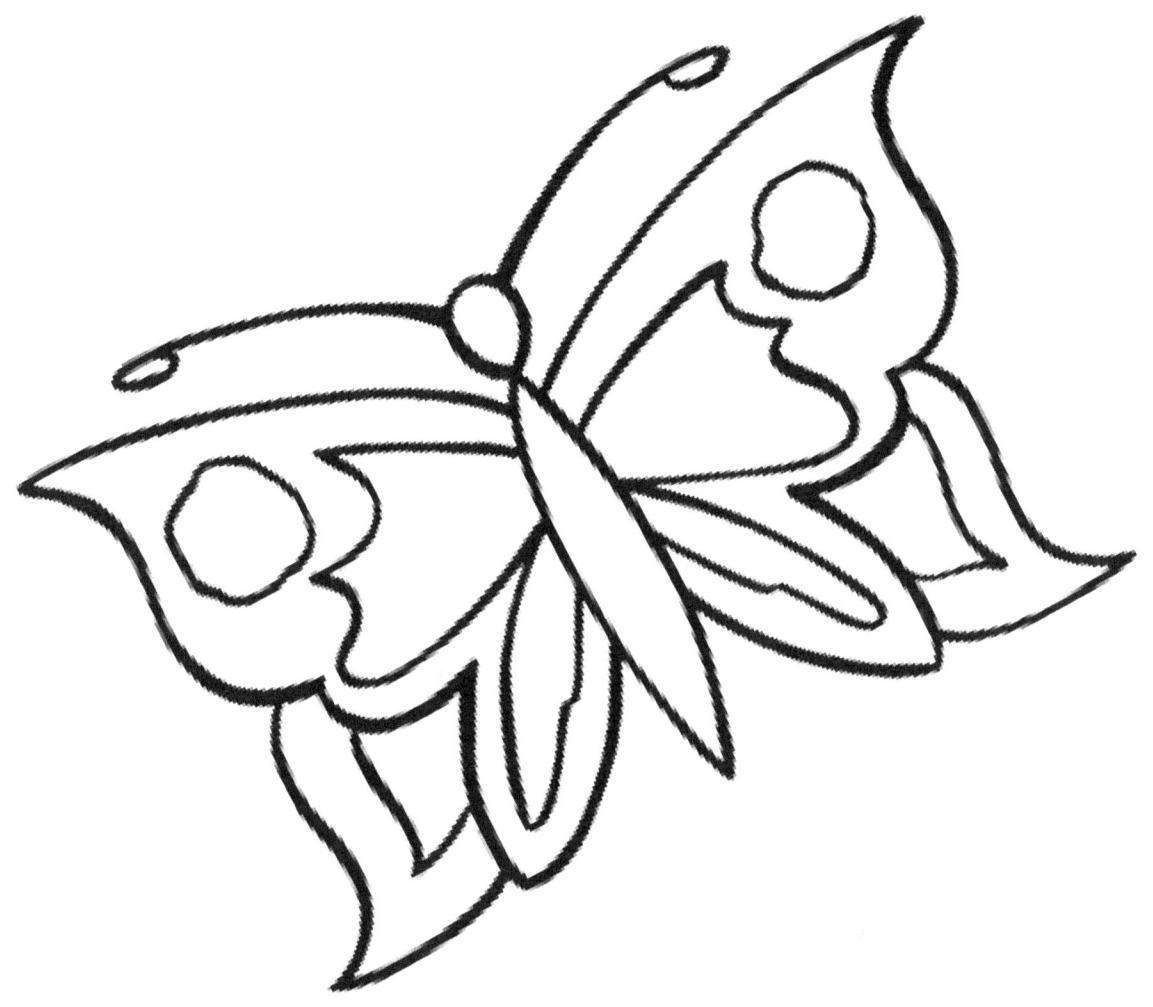

Make this Butterfly Beautiful!!!!

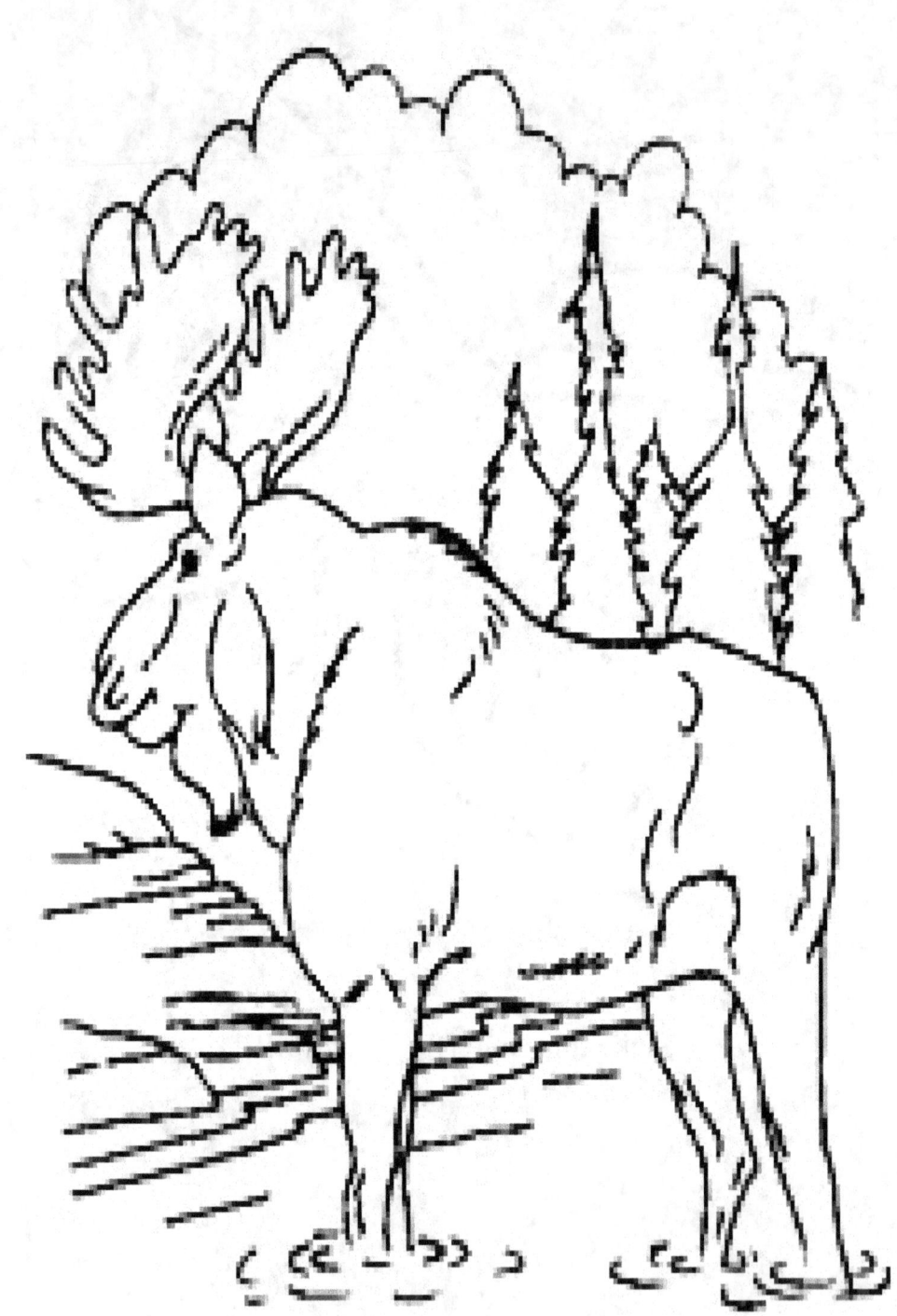

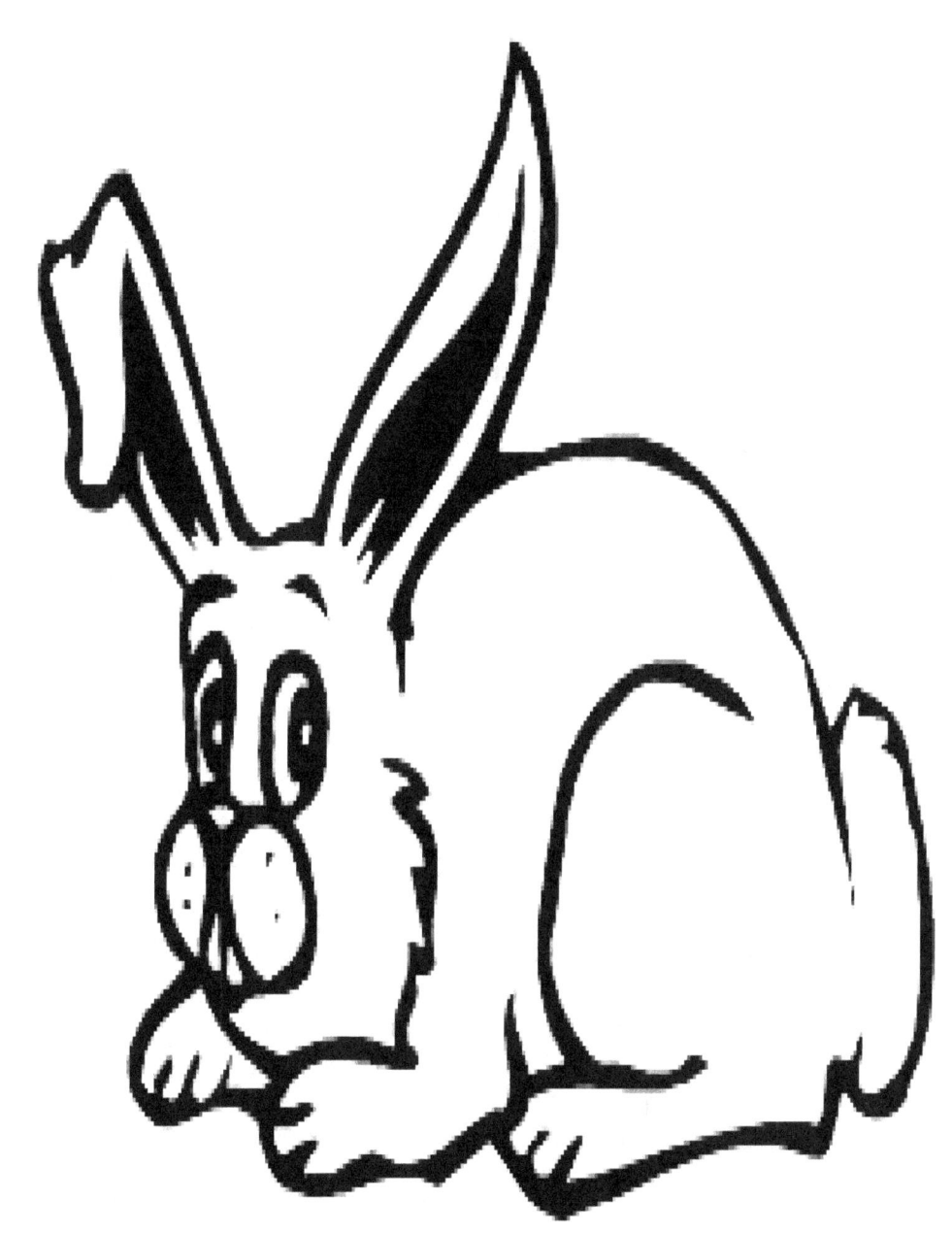

Bunnies go HOP HOP HOPPIN!

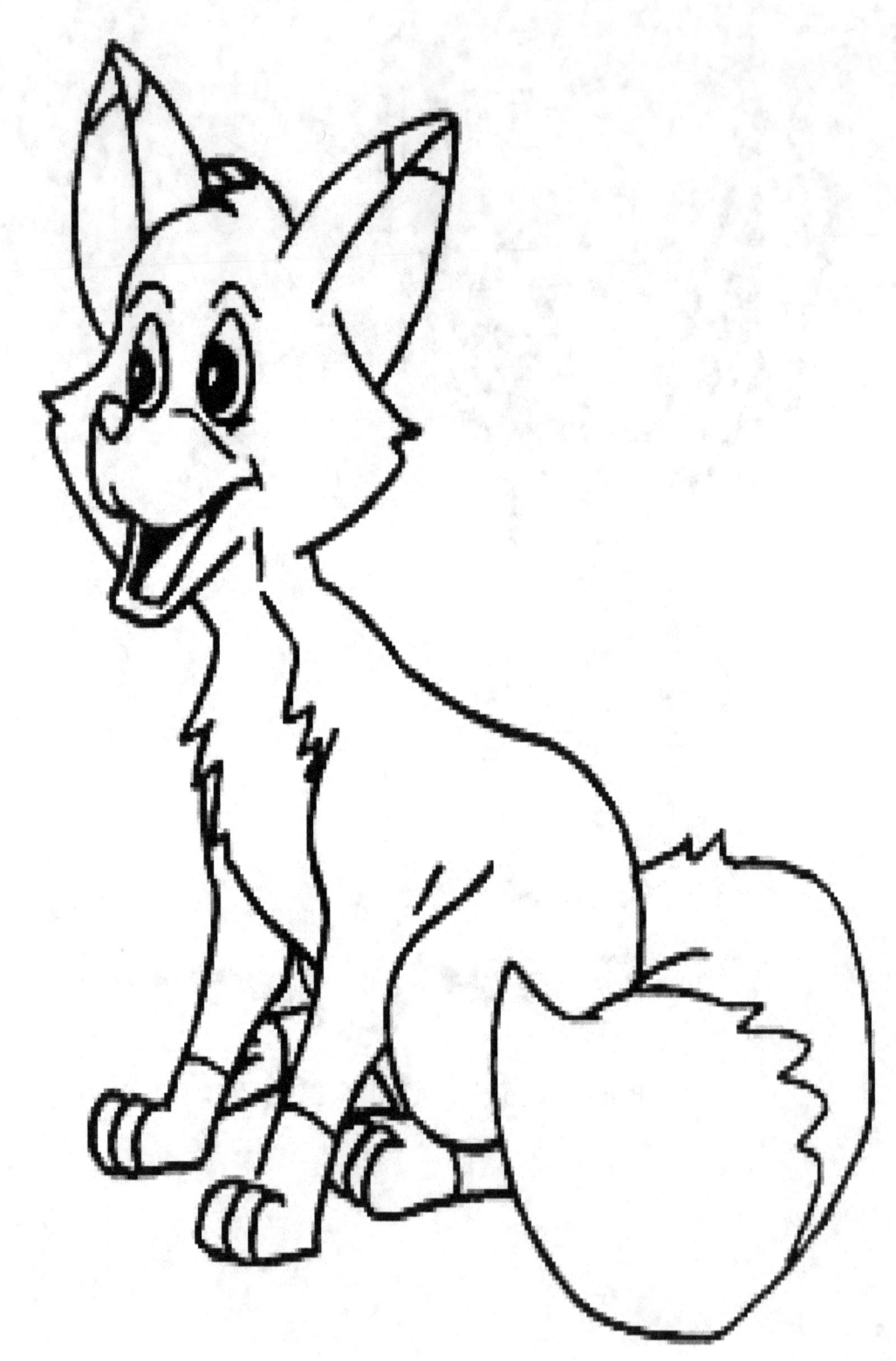

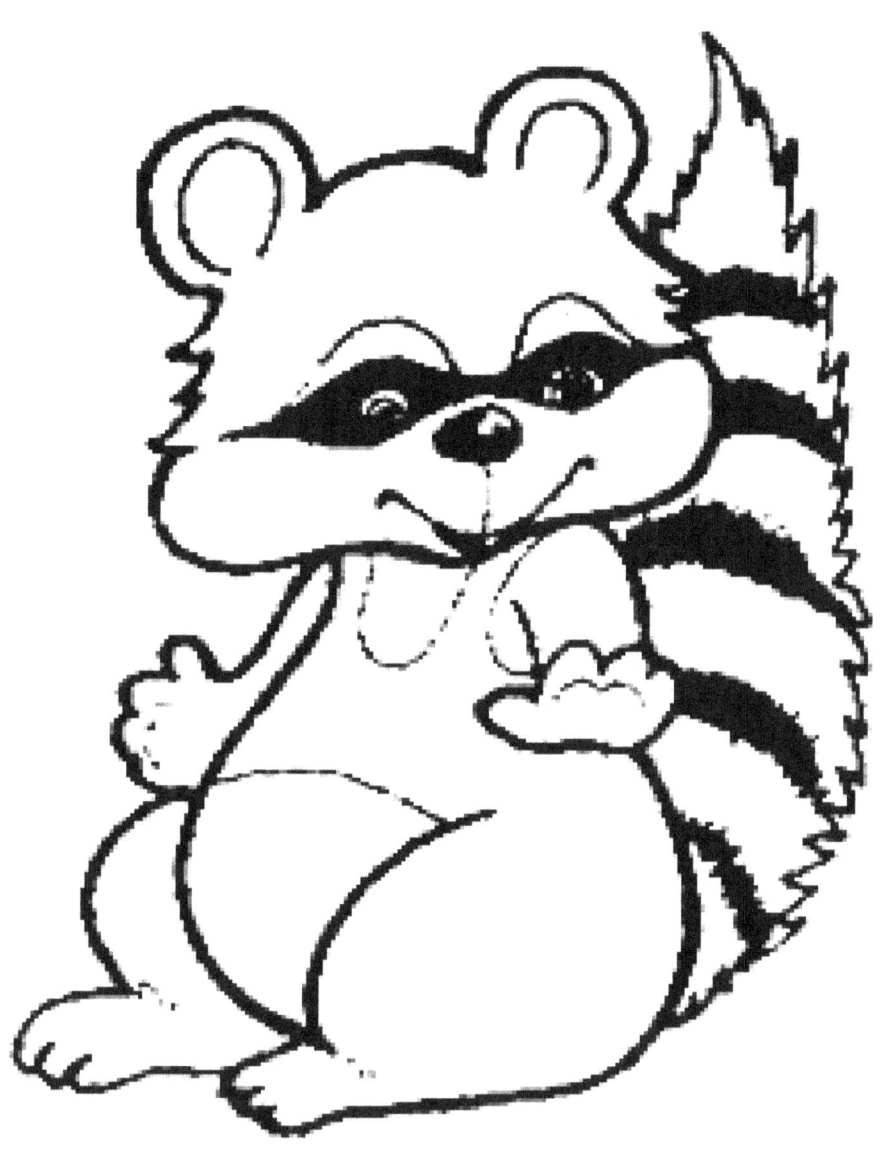

Meet Wally the Raccoon!

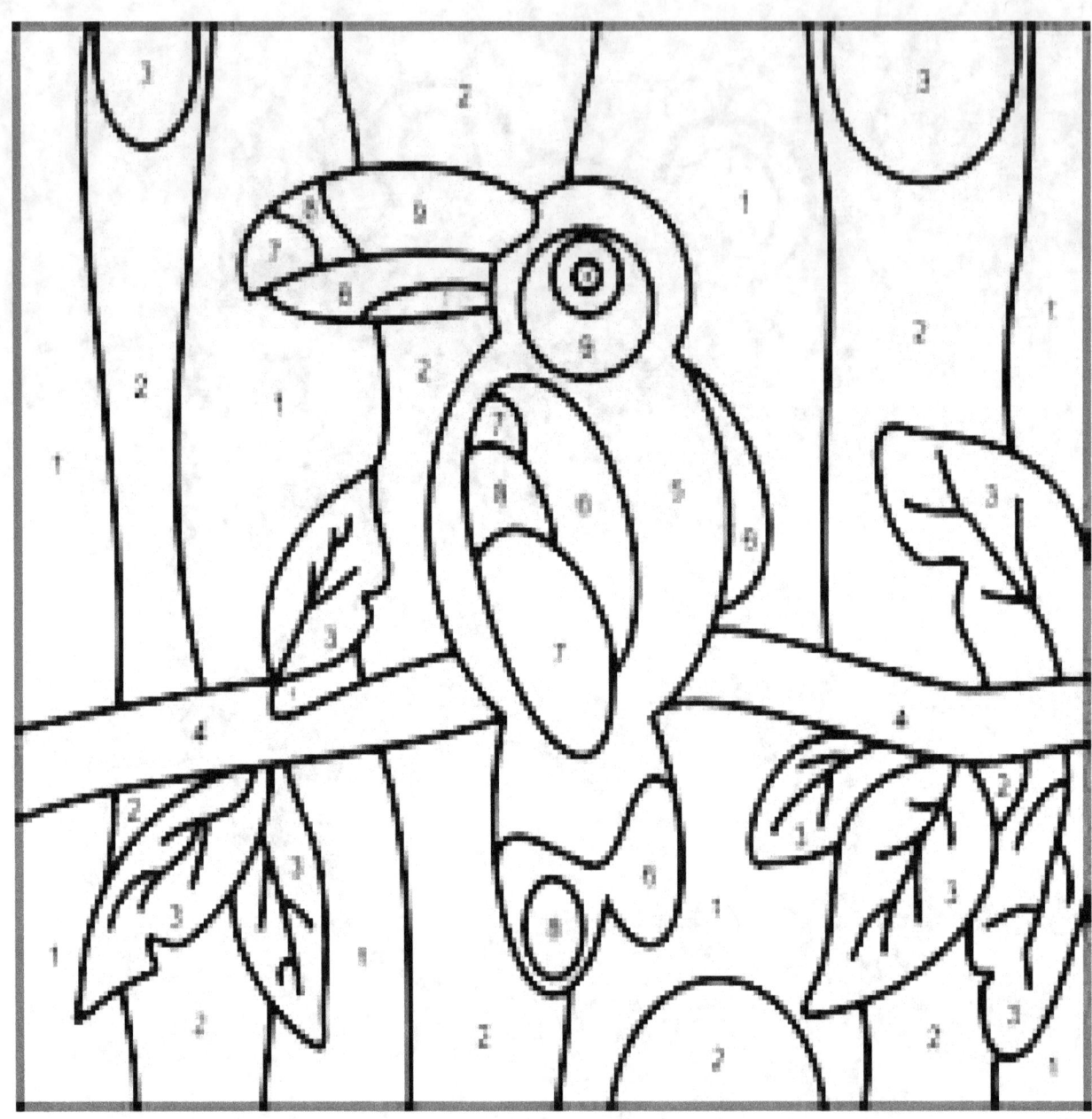

Pick a color for each number see what you get!

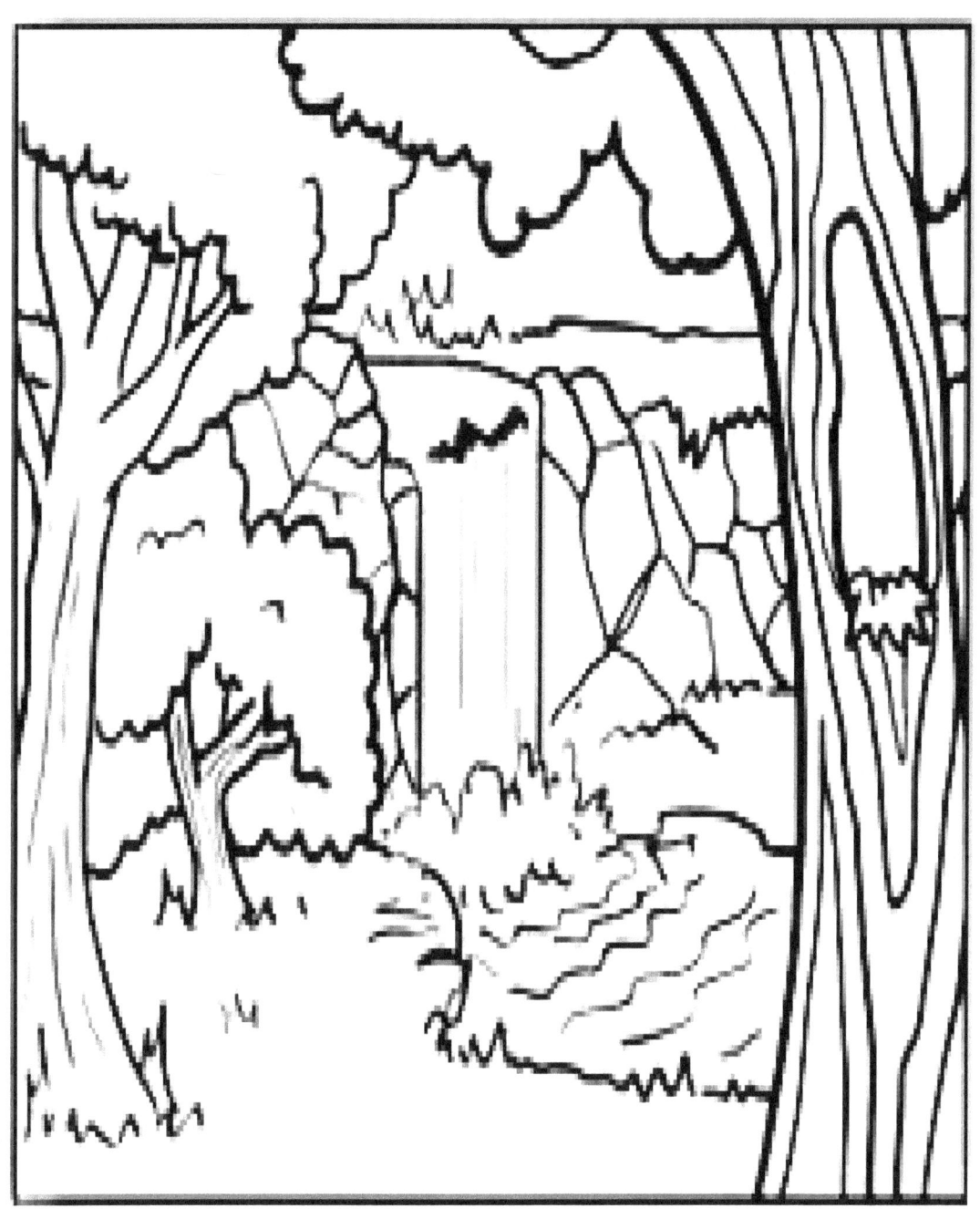

Draw you a wild animal!

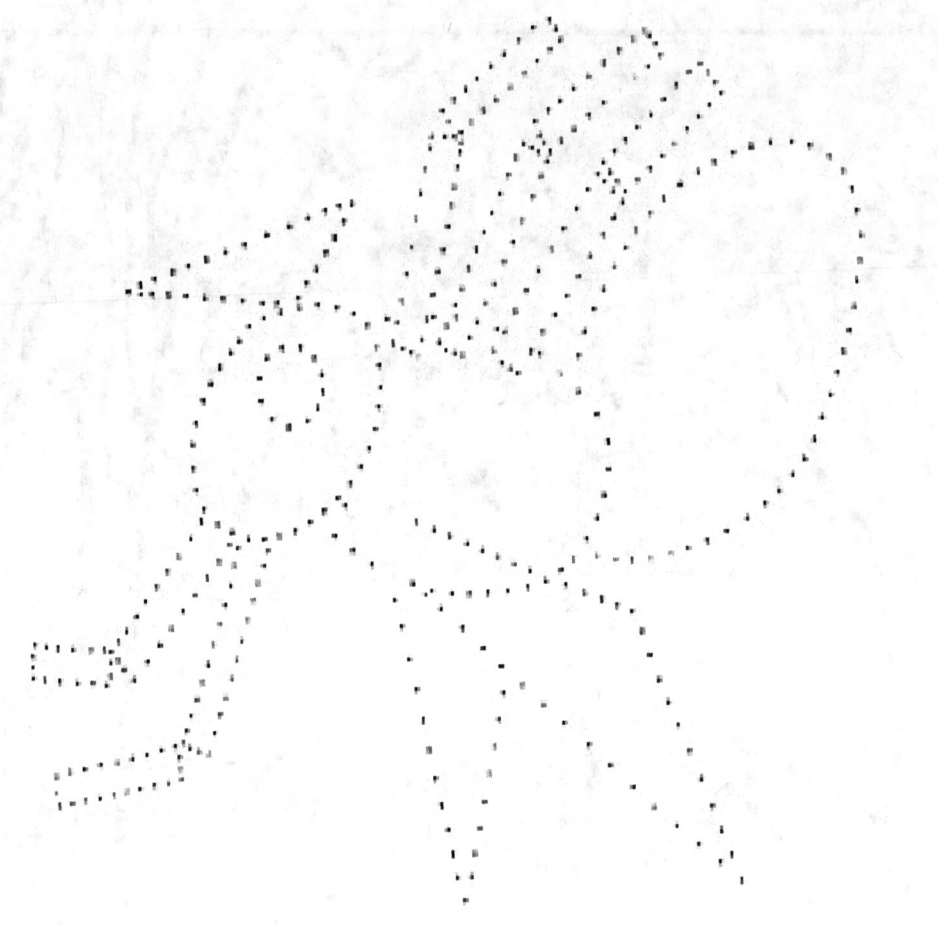

Trace and Color!

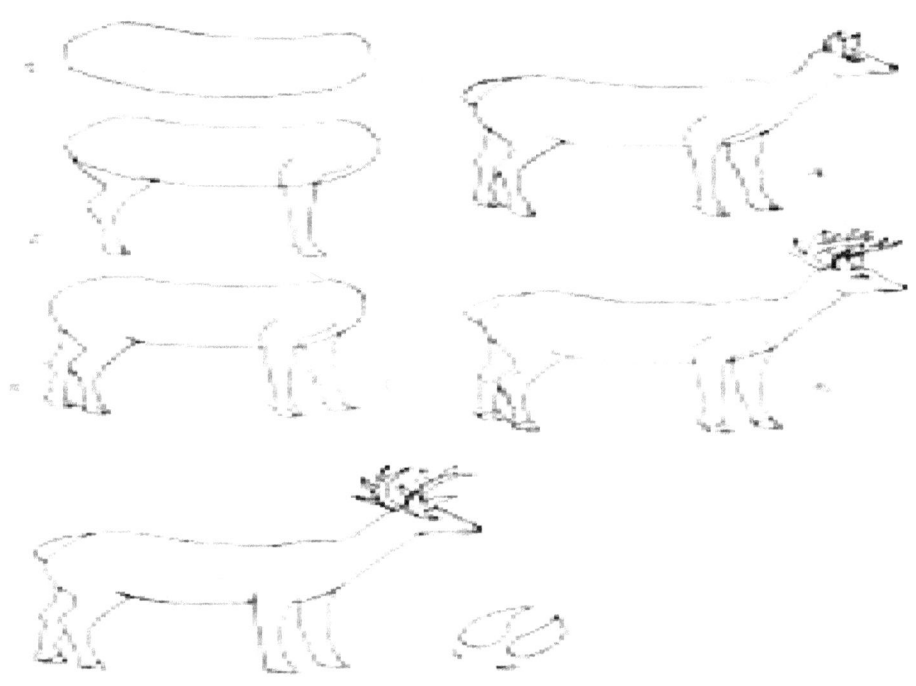

See If you can follow the steps and draw you a DEER!

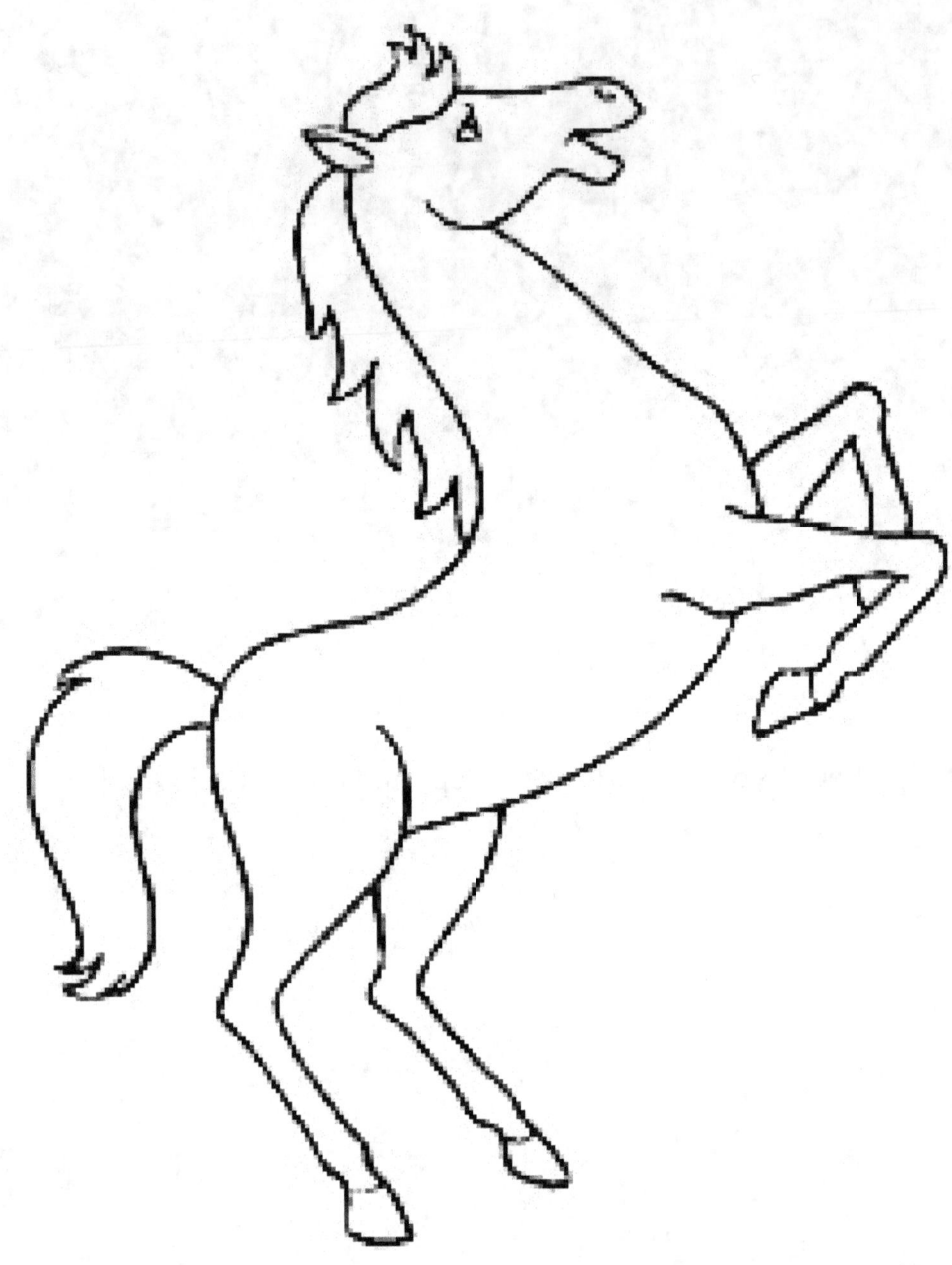

Wild Horses are Beautiful!

What Color Would You Like Yours to be?

www.ingramcontent.com/pod-product-compliance
Lightning Source LLC
Chambersburg PA
CBHW082303200526
45168CB00017B/2766